# The Spiritual Path of Nonviolent Communication

# *The* Spiritual Path *of* Nonviolent Communication

## Living with Compassion, Connection & Understanding

**ROBERT GONZALES**

**Edited by Lynd Morris**

SHAMBHALA

Shambhala Publications, Inc.
2129 13th Street
Boulder, Colorado 80302
www.shambhala.com



Cover art: Marina Zlochin/Adobe Stock
Cover design: Daniel Urban-Brown
Interior design: Laura Shaw Design



9 8 7 6 5 4 3 2 1

First Edition
Printed in the United States of America

Shambhala Publications makes every effort to print on acid-free, recycled paper.
Shambhala Publications is distributed worldwide by Penguin Random House, Inc., and its subsidiaries.

Library of Congress Cataloging-in-Publication Data
Names: Gonzales, Robert, 1949–2021 author
Title: The spiritual path of nonviolent communication: living with compassion, connection, and understanding / Robert Gonzales; edited by Lynd Morris.
Description: First edition. | Boulder, Colorado: Shambhala, [2026] | Includes bibliographical references.
Identifiers: LCCN 2025023267 | ISBN 9781645474340 trade paperback
Subjects: LCSH: Interpersonal communication | Interpersonal relations | Compassion | Spiritual life
Classification: LCC BF637.C45 G645 2026
LC record available at https://lccn.loc.gov/2025023267

The authorized representative in the EU for product safety and compliance is eucomply OÜ, Pärnu mnt 139b-14, 11317 Tallinn, Estonia, hello@eucompliancepartner.com.

The Living Compassion website: http://living-compassion.org

---

There are signs everywhere,
there are guides everywhere,
inner and outer.
In order to see the signs
and follow the guides, this is required:
Listen . . . and feel . . . very carefully.
You must stop and take your time
because the signs are everywhere, in everything,
inner and outer.

Celebrate the presence of the Holy when you feel it,
let it overtake you.
Let it leave you breathless . . . in awe
at the sheer, never-ending Beauty.
be surprised by Grace . . . it is everywhere,
and in every moment.

Find friends on your journey.
Feed each other, nurture each other,
inspire each other, play with each other.
In the feeding, nurturing, inspiring, and play,
heaven is revealed and lived.
Then, relaxing, surrender into the grace of gratitude,
letting the energy do its work on you.
Let us go on this journey in life together.
Join me.

---

—Excerpted from “Heaven Is Here” by Robert Gonzales

# Contents

# Foreword

AS LONG AS I KNEW ROBERT, he was always passionate about contributing to the well-being of others. Through his courses and work with countless individuals, he guided transformation, healing, and awakening in those around him. I was privileged to be at Robert's side throughout his last twenty-eight years. During this time, Robert loved and supported our family unconditionally. I experienced great joy as he shared his insights with me, and I observed them come alive in his interactions with our children and grandchildren. It was a gift to witness Robert develop his life practice into the work of Living Compassion and to see him bring that to the world.

Robert was always guided by an inner knowing and deeper wisdom. He had a profound spiritual experience as a child that formed and informed his life—an event described on page 111. The insights he shared throughout his life always came from his own experiences. He would spend long periods of time in reflection, connecting inwardly to what only he could describe, the wisdom that fueled his life and teachings.

Robert lived what he taught. He embodied Living Compassion. He lived fully present to all of his experiences. Watching him accept and embrace even that which was emotionally uncomfortable or painful was an example of and inspiration for what is possible. Even in the midst of the most challenging experiences, I saw his ability to be authentic, vulnerable, and honest with himself as a deep commitment to self-love and care. Robert knew the power of being fully present to life. His practice of this inspired others and informed his work.

I am deeply grateful to the team of people who have brought Robert's words into book form to be available to a greater number of people. The information and the processes offered here carry deeper truths that welcome us to return to them over time. I invite you to come back to this book periodically. In revisiting Robert's insights, I believe understanding and experiences deepen, and the connection to our authentic selves strengthens, making our lives richer and more fulfilling. I have seen how the information presented here has healed and transformed lives. It has mine.

May this book guide you to the beauty of your own heart.

—**RUTH JOY,**
*beloved wife of Robert Gonzales*

# Preface

THIS BOOK IS BASED on the online program "The Spirituality of Nonviolent Communication: A Course in Living Compassion." It was offered from October to December 2020 by the international Nonviolent Communication (NVC) teacher and Living Compassion developer Robert Gonzales. After publishing *Reflections on Living Compassion: Awakening Our Passion and Living in Compassion* in 2015, Robert decided to create a series of books sharing his life work of Living Compassion, and the 2020 online program—intended for those who'd already participated in five or more days of NVC training—was to become the basis for the first book in that series. Sadly, Robert passed away before he was able to make these publications a reality. However, some dedicated friends and colleagues have taken up this project to realize Robert's vision for sharing his work and contributing to more people's lives. Robert's teachings have transformed each of our lives, and we want others to benefit from them, too. We are among many of Robert's students who have offered his Living Compassion practices around the world. His legacy lives on.

This book is about the way Robert conceptualized living into the principles of NVC within and between us, something he called "a twofold spiritual life practice for Living Compassion," which he described as the spiritual basis of Nonviolent Communication. When promoting his online course, Robert said, "This material is an invitation to develop a foundational consciousness. To fully empower our place in life, we must first cultivate and strengthen our center from which we engage with life. When we act from our center, fueled by love, we start to harness a force that is beyond what we've known is possible."

In memory of Robert's life and his outstanding contributions to the world, and in loving service to making his teachings available for all, we present you with *The Spiritual Path of Nonviolent Communication: Living with Compassion, Connection, and Understanding*. We have attempted to keep as close to Robert's actual words as possible to convey his presence to you. We trust this will be as profoundly meaningful a journey with Robert for you as it has been—and is—for us.

LYND MORRIS (United States)
FILIPA HOPE (New Zealand)
SIMONE ANLIKER (Switzerland)
BETT FARBER (United States)

*For more information about the publication team, see pages 125–27.*

# Editor's Introduction

"YOU'VE GOT TO MEET ROBERT GONZALES," my friend urged as we neared the end of the 2005 North American Nonviolent Communication (NVC) Leadership Program. "I think he has what you are looking for."

What was I looking for?

In my twenties, I looked for something that would make sense of my world and help me feel at home, no matter where I was. I discovered meditation and did my best to cultivate a peaceful practice.

In my thirties, I became a mom, and I looked for ways to experience peace (and quiet) at home and in the workplace.

In my forties, I discovered mindfulness practice, and I looked for opportunities to live every moment mindfully. My teacher, Thich Nhat Hanh, said that listening deeply and speaking compassionately was part of this practice. While I worked diligently to express myself with kindness and care, I was baffled about how to listen to others so I could hear not only what they were saying but also what was being left unsaid. What exactly was I trying to hear?

Fortunately, in my fifties, I was introduced to Nonviolent Communication (NVC). Here, at last, were clear and effective tools for hearing the essence of what I and others were trying to communicate and for expressing myself so others could hear what was most important to me.

While growing greater skills throughout the lengthy process of NVC trainer certification, I found myself wanting to integrate NVC (also called Compassionate Communication) practices with spiritual practices to create peace at home and in the world. But where could I find a mentor and a community of people who shared my vision for spiritually based communication? It was this quest that led my friend to urge me to meet Robert Gonzales, an international NVC trainer known for his unique spiritual approach to living and sharing Compassionate Communication.

My friend was right.

From my first retreat with Robert Gonzales, I experienced the vibrancy of his loving presence, his depth of listening, and his profound insight into life. I sensed immediately that Robert Gonzales really did have what I was looking for.

Robert's work emerged from a lifetime of inquiry into the intersection between spirituality and human communication. He was born in Arizona and moved as a child to Southern California, where he grew up, went to college and received a PhD in clinical psychology, and practiced as a therapist—offering individual and couples counseling—for many years. In 1985, Robert met Dr. Marshall Rosenberg, the gifted leader in communication and conflict resolution who developed NVC's key principles and practices in the 1960s.

Dr. Rosenberg based NVC on the principle of ahimsa, which he described as "the natural state of compassion when no violence is present in the heart." Expressing ourselves honestly and listening with empathy are fundamental NVC skills, according to Dr. Rosenberg, and he created a model for listening and speaking that supports deep connection with ourselves and others. Framing what we hear and say using observations, feelings, needs, and requests (see pages xix–xxi for a brief description of how this model is used in practice), we are better able to remember our intention to be present and to discern what gets in the way of this.

Within a year of meeting Dr. Rosenberg, Robert began offering NVC trainings to students, church congregations, social workers, psychologists, mediators, and public groups. He became a certified NVC trainer and contributed to the global Center for Nonviolent Communication (CNVC) founded by Dr. Rosenberg as a lead trainer for NVC International Intensive Training programs, as the president of the board of directors for CNVC, and as an assessor for certifying trainers. Robert cofounded the NVC Training Institute with a team of international NVC trainers, and they offered retreats in the United States and Europe that provided in-depth and continuing NVC training.

In 2006 Robert launched the NVC LIFE (Living and Integrating Full Embodiment) program, a multiyear advanced intensive study program designed to deepen and integrate a needs awareness into everyday life. The LIFE Program was so transformative that within just a few years, long waiting lists formed to participate in these trainings, which Robert offered in the United States, Europe, and Australia.

I learned from Marshall Rosenberg how to communicate an awareness of life-serving needs. I learned from Robert how to take that awareness to a much deeper level, not only recognizing needs but also directly experiencing the animating life energy behind needs as they arise in everyone. Through Robert I found a community of people learning how to listen deeply and speak compassionately from a place of union with all of life.

In 2009, Robert invited five LIFE students who were sharing his practices in their own communities to join him at a series of private retreats to clarify the principles of what became the culmination of his life's work and his greatest legacy: Living Compassion. We clarified the five core principles of Living Compassion, which Robert addresses in this book:

There is only one life energy.

Every action is an expression of this life energy.

All suffering results from the obstruction of this life flow.

Compassion liberates the energy caught in suffering and this produces healing.

When this energy is liberated, it naturally goes into life seeking communion, community, connection, and belonging.

In 2010, Robert founded the Center for Living Compassion, through which he offered Living Compassion seminars and retreats—in person and online—to thousands of people until his passing in November 2021. In Robert's words,

> My work with Living Compassion emerges from my own inner journey enriched and inspired by many that I have enjoyed being and working with. What I share is centered in the dimension of the heart; it is what is most deeply alive in me and the most meaningful activity in my life.

Robert's message of spiritual deepening through relationship with others lives on through the network of people who continue to offer Living Compassion courses in several languages around the world, in person and via Zoom. (See the Living Compassion website at www.living-compassion.org for more information.) You will also experience Robert's insight and inspiration through this book, *The Spiritual Path of Nonviolent Communication: Living with Compassion, Connection, and Understanding*, which is based on one of the final online courses he offered prior to his death. In it he distills his concepts for how to live the principles of NVC within us and between us. He calls this "a twofold spiritual life practice for living compassion," and he describes it as the spiritual basis of NVC. When promoting this online course, Robert said,

> This material is an invitation to develop a foundational consciousness. To fully empower our place in life, we must first cultivate and strengthen our center from which we engage with life. When we act from our center, fueled by love, we start to harness a force that is beyond what we've known is possible.

*The Spiritual Path of Nonviolent Communication: Living with Compassion, Connection, and Understanding* is a portal through which

Robert has communicated with warmth and wisdom the concepts and practices he developed to guide people into a direct and embodied experience of Living Compassion. The energy of heart, mind, and spirit you will encounter as you read this book is the energy that informed his entire life.

You now have the opportunity to meet Robert Gonzales. Perhaps you'll find what you are looking for, too.

—**LYND MORRIS,**
Silver Spring, Maryland, April 2025

# A Taste of Nonviolent Communication

NONVIOLENT COMMUNICATION—usually referred to as NVC or Compassionate Communication—is a set of principles and processes that have been used successfully in many countries around the world to create understanding, foster compassion, and transform conflict into connection between individuals and groups, and even within our own internal conflicts.

The primary intention for practicing NVC is to connect with our own humanity and the humanity in others. Two fundamental NVC premises are that (1) everything every human being does is intended to meet needs (whether or not this is successful), and (2) everyone's needs are equally valued.

The practice of NVC has two parts: expressing what is important to you, and listening for what is most important to others as they try to communicate. The NVC founder Dr. Rosenberg created a model to make communicating authentically and compassionately a simple process for those speaking and those listening. The NVC model has four steps.

### AN NVC DIALOGUE

1. Make **observations** instead of evaluations or judgments (i.e., saying, "You did not get home when you said you would" instead of "You are always late!").

2. Identify the **feelings** (including sensations and emotions) that are present, being careful not to confuse these with beliefs or interpretations (i.e., saying, "I feel sad and lonely" instead of "I feel like you abandoned me").

3. Guess which life-serving **needs** might be giving rise to the feelings arising in yourself or the other person before even considering strategies to meet those needs (i.e., saying, "I value order and simplicity" instead of "I need you to pick up your clothes.").

4. Make **requests** of yourself or someone else to ensure the feelings and needs that were expressed have been understood (i.e., saying, "How does this sound to you?" or "Were my guesses about what's important to you close?") or to suggest a specific positive action instead of issuing a demand (i.e., saying, "Would you be willing to call me when you get home?" instead of "Call me as soon as you arrive!").

Although each of these steps facilitates genuine connection between people, an NVC dialogue is not necessarily linear, and even if one or more steps are occasionally omitted, step 3 will always be included: listening for (and expressing) the nourishing values and needs at the heart of whatever we are trying to communicate.

This taste of NVC is intended to help those new to the practice to understand the references to it in this book. However, there are numerous excellent resources that provide opportunities to explore the principles behind the NVC practices. *Nonviolent Communication: A Language for Life* by Dr. Rosenberg is a particularly clear, inspiring, and even entertaining introduction to NVC, and it includes examples and practices in each chapter that can be done alone or with a partner.

According to the global Center for Nonviolent Communication, there are nearly a thousand certified trainers teaching NVC in more than sixty-five countries. Even more people offer NVC practices informally. Many special forms of the NVC dialogue have been developed to enhance communication with family members, friends, colleagues, or even strangers, regardless of the setting and whether what is being expressed is appreciation, disappointment, frustration, regret, affection, or anything else. When people know they've been heard with respect and openness, they are often more able to listen with respect and openness. In this way, NVC—a language for life—is also a language for connection, understanding, and peace.

For more information, visit the global Center for Nonviolent Communication website (https://www.cnvc.org/) to find in-person or online NVC training. And see the NVC Academy website (https://nvcacademy.com/) to access more than 1,200 live and prerecorded NVC courses and other resources for all experience levels in a wide range to topics, including an entire section devoted to Robert Gonzales that includes more than one hundred hours of his course recordings.

# The Spiritual Path of Nonviolent Communication

CHAPTER ONE

# The Heart of Spirituality

THE DIVINE IS A MYSTERY. It is unknowable and beyond qualities. It has no boundaries. It is infinite beyond any kind of conception. It is absolute in every moment, thing, and element of existence. It is everything and not any one thing. There is a no-thingness to this mystery. It is formless and imbued in every moment of existence and every form of being. Being is protruding from infinity as all things, from apparent nothing, blooming into glorious everything.

Sometimes this mystery is called "emptiness." Sometimes it is called "all that is." Sometimes it is called "Reality" or "God." Whatever it is called, it is the very essence and fabric of existence, manifesting in every molecule and particle, greater and beyond every form of its manifestation. So close, it is closer than close. So obvious, it is hidden from most, except those who have received the grace of recognition.

Where this mystery—infinite, eternal, beyond all qualities and yet in every fiber of our Being—meets manifest life in its most pure form, there is exquisite, ineffable beauty, compassion, and peace.

For most of us, this awe-inspiring, alive presence is obscured. Those who are graced or blessed feel it as a yearning. Those who are vulnerable to the great power of this mystery have been blessed with its presence in the mystery of their living. They live in awe, joy, freedom, love, and peace. Those who have had the courage to utterly surrender with eyes wide open to the ocean of life, the power of mystery, have no self. They experience only the existence of the body-mind as an instrument of the music that this mystery plays.

---

These words came to me several years ago. They express what, for me, is most meaningful and essential in the word *spirituality*, what the construct of spirituality points to. This book is about living in the heart of spirituality, living in freedom and fullness. It is a book about a human spirituality that is lived inwardly, internally, and in relationships in everyday life. It is a book about Living Compassion.

The notion of spirituality is rooted in the premise that there is a spiritual dimension to our existence that manifests subjectively and intersubjectively, within and between. There is an "I" and a "we" to living, and it is the integration of these two dimensions of life that are the focus of the work I call Living Compassion. It's not only practical but also enriching to enhance and embody these two dimensions, as we exist in our daily lives, both individually and in the space of our relationships. On a very practical level, the integration of these dimensions brings the notion of fullness into our everyday life.

One of the ways to approach the meaning of spirituality is that it is essential in life and touches the spirit of what a human being is. It has nothing to do with belief systems, dogma, or religion. The meaning I assign to the word *spirituality* is not contained by those conceptual systems. It is something that is universal.

The notion of spirituality in the context of Nonviolent Communication (NVC) is that we bring our deep individuality, our deep identity, into interbeing. To do this requires a necessary set of consciousness, skills, and capacities. One without the other is not complete. For me, the interior, individual, subjective spirituality is not complete unless I include the intersubjective, the life that exists between each living being, in our relational spaces. Qualities such as compassion, honesty, and integrity are manifestations or functions of living our Being in relationships, something that can be called "the Divine." Spirituality of this sort is available to us at every moment. In life, whenever there is kindness, understanding, compassion, and deep, equal mattering, the Divine is present, because those are the qualities of the Divine. There are many transformational processes and pointers that can support us in embodying these qualities.

## THE NVC DOORWAY TO SPIRITUALITY

How does this notion of spirituality relate to the practice and process of NVC?

NVC provides an efficient template for a dramatic shift from the common mindsets of judgment, blame, and criticism that are at the root of suffering, toward authentic honesty and empathic connection with self and others. There is a lot to be said about the skills and language that NVC invites us into. If we don't have the precision and clarity of our language, this is like having a musical instrument that is not tuned. NVC provides a language as a way of tuning our communication.

But NVC is so much more than a communication technique.

It's easy at the beginning levels to learn and practice NVC as a mechanical process—sometimes people call these the four steps of making observations, identifying feelings, guessing needs, and then making requests—and if they follow these steps, they believe they are communicating.

But if we only use these four steps, we are missing the essential part of NVC, the heart and soul of this communication process, which is really none other than the heart and soul of each of us as human beings.

We need to have a genuine intention to connect to the other human being, from heart to heart. Without that intention, NVC can easily digress into manipulation, into a mechanical practice of a process that uses a certain kind of jargon and isn't fully alive and human.

We have all been conditioned and subjected to a kind of learning that is centered in our head—thinking about the "rightness" and the "wrongness" of our behavior or other people's behavior, what's good and what's evil, what's appropriate and what's inappropriate, what's rude and what's polite. These judgments come from our mind. And very often these judgments create a kind of polarization where we push the other person away. Often the kind of judgments we have justifies punishment or reward.

NVC gives us a different kind of language. We call it a language of the heart. We can start to see that this judgmental thinking and language alienates us from the natural condition of the human heart. The training in NVC is to recognize that kind of thinking and to witness it. This is the ability to make an observation and to differentiate this from evaluations and interpretations.

Another basic NVC skill is the ability to identify feelings and to experience their felt sense. For me, feelings are an expression of the life energy flowing through us. When we allow ourselves to fully feel, we are connecting with the living, vibrant energy of life. This connection is not just emotional but deeply spiritual, as it allows us to access a more authentic and present experience of our Being.

A sensation is not an emotion. There are two levels of sensation. One I call "dense" or "gross," such as physical tension or tightness in the way a muscle is tight. The other is a more subtle form of sensation, a finer vibration of physical energy, like a whirling in the solar plexus that is a sensation, not an emotion. We may feel an emotion, but the physical part of the emotion is an energy that is felt on a subtler level. Sensation is vital in the practice of being aware of what is happening in the present moment. Noticing sensation can be a doorway to liberation from suffering, as it grounds us in the reality of the moment rather than in the stories our minds create.

Feelings are valuable indicators, but they are not the essence of what is alive in me. For me, the most important aspect of NVC is the concept of universal human needs. Needs are qualities that we experience internally, such as understanding, support, or connection, while strategies are the choices we make to meet those needs. A strategy is a specific thing we do, but the need is the underlying energy we hope to fulfill through that action.

Needs are the heart of the NVC process, and the consciousness of needs is the beginning of the spiritual dimension within it. Needs are those qualities or values that are universal. Needs are what make us human. When we truly see another's needs, we see their humanity. Needs can also be described as "values" or "universal life energies" such as love, sustenance. I remember Marshall Rosenberg, the founder of NVC, often describing needs as the energy of life reaching for life. We all have access to this animating energy within us that is always reaching for life. It emerges or emanates from our true self, our very essence. In this sense, I see spirituality as our relationship to the life force. And I see "life force" as the energy that emerges or emanates from our true Being and manifests as our human needs.

Those who have studied spirituality through the wisdom traditions are familiar with the concept of the essential Being. The notion of the true self runs throughout the spiritual traditions. The ultimate goal of these traditions is awakening, self-realization, or enlightenment, which transforms our identity from a separate self to wholeness. Our true nature as human beings is that we are loving, compassionate, and innately free.

The interior, embodied consciousness is the spirituality within. NVC invites us to live our spirituality as an embodied experience. When we can truly connect to the energy of our needs, we feel them in our whole body, including neurologically and cellularly, and it nourishes us.

The way we can feel and access the true self—the spiritual core of our Being—is through these qualities of needs. One of the many ways to experience the qualities of our Being more directly is through the longings of our heart. This is accessible to everyone. Our longings can take many different forms, and they are all felt in and through the heart.

We long for understanding. We long for respect and dignity. We long for honesty and authenticity. We long for love and support. When we get in touch with the longings of our heart, we can access our core values in life. Something that is of deep value is an aspect of our true selves.

One of the strengths and benefits of NVC is that it identifies many specific and concretely available qualities that we call universal human needs. These needs are longings that unfold from the core of our Being. The spirituality of NVC is rooted in our needs because they connect us to our essence. Life force emanates from our essence; it moves in and through us, and it manifests and expresses through our longings, through our needs, and through what we value.

One description of needs that I enjoy is: *They are the holes in heaven through which God's light shines*. This is how I have experienced and made sense of the spirituality of Nonviolent Communication through the heart of our universal human needs.

When we touch a deep need and feel it, we are much more empowered when we make a request because its power comes from this energy of the beautiful need. In my experience, people will respond to a request in a life-serving way when they are connected to our need and not to the energy of managing and controlling. "This is what I would enjoy" is an invitation that says "I don't have to have my request met. I completely respect your choice about whatever needs you are meeting." NVC helps us make these distinctions, and it helps us to direct our life energy. Further, NVC helps us come to a full connection with someone by directing that life energy in the form of the present, doable requests we make of them.

The objective of Nonviolent Communication is to connect with other human beings in a way in which our human needs and values and the other person's are equally valued. When we can connect on this level, something dramatic happens in us. There is a shift in which we are then willing to give and receive mutually from the heart.

## A DEEPER LOOK: WHAT IS LIVING COMPASSION?

As my exploration of NVC and spirituality deepened over the years, a clarity emerged about ways to cultivate a daily practice—with myself and in relationship with others—that compassionately embraces all of life. This led me to develop practical pathways for a daily spiritual practice—Living Compassion—that offers processes and inner maps for living in the fullness and flow of life.

Understanding the conceptual framework of Living Compassion can support us in experiencing it. Concepts are important when they lead to direct experience, but if they just stay intellectual concepts, they don't do a lot of good. We can think about compassion as a concept, but that's different from living it. When we *embody* a quality, we are living it. When we are living a quality fully, we are inhabiting it; we become it. We can cultivate and develop the capacity to live compassion, to become it. The intention of this work is to live compassion by meeting whatever arises with it.

It's also important to understand what I mean by "compassion." For me, compassion is a state of my inner Being that cannot be measured and doesn't have boundaries. It is not limited; it doesn't have a beginning, a middle, or an end. It is something that is present and experienceable but not graspable. When our experiences are met with this all-allowing, all-accepting, and unconditional experience of compassion, they are transformed.

During the years I've offered Living Compassion, it has become clear that five core principles create its underlying foundation or context. These core principles form the fundamental orientation of Living Compassion that always points toward aliveness, toward the underlying beauty of everything. Each one of these principles has profound implications, so this is just a brief summary of them.

### *The First Core Principle*

The first core principle as I've identified it is this: There is only one life energy, one life force that is all-encompassing and permeates life on all levels. It manifests into the multiplicity and diversity of all other forms of expression, but fundamentally there is only one. This may seem simple and obvious, but the implication of this is that in life there is a totality that is sometimes called "source" or "all that is" or "that which is." Out of this mystery of *what is* comes that one cohesive life force.

*The Second Core Principle*

The second core principle of Living Compassion is that this life force animates everything; it is the source of all of life, and it moves in every aspect of life, manifesting in the physical world, the biological world, and the human world. This life force moves in and through every human being. Everything that human beings say and do is an expression of this life energy.

The life force manifests through the human heart as particular longings and yearnings that in NVC we call "universal human needs." These are the vital qualities that all human beings value and are motivated by. Although we have no control over the existence of the life force that is powerful and immense beyond our thought or imagination, what we can do is to open to the qualities of beauty, love, and tender care that are inherent in it.

*The Third Core Principle*

The third principle has to do with what happens when there is an obstacle or a constriction to the life force. In human beings, this results in suffering. One way this suffering manifests is the experience of separation in which we feel ourselves separated from our essential Being and other human beings. Another way suffering manifests is through surviving, protecting, and defending. We create the protective and survival structures that we identify with, out of which comes the fundamental language of judgment; the language of right and wrong, good and bad.

As we grow up, our traumatic experiences and cultural conditioning create a set of beliefs that we identify with. Anytime we experience reactivity and find ourselves in a suffering, contracted state of fear, survival is at its core. For example, "I'm right, and you're wrong!" and "That's inappropriate!" are both expressions of survival.

*The Fourth Core Principle*

When there is suffering—disconnection or life alienation—in our inner life or our relationships, we can bring compassion to this, and the life force that has been blocked is released and transformed so that it can manifest in life. This energy can only be liberated when we receive compassion from another or when we offer it to ourselves. That is the fourth principle: When compassion is brought to the constriction of suffering, it releases and reveals the life energy held captive. Compassion doesn't get rid of the pain, but it reveals that which is precious in the heart of the pain. At the very heart of each particle of suffering is precious life energy that has been held captive by our tendencies to protect and survive.

Whether we experience compassion for the suffering within us or within another human being, this quality of awareness that is all-encompassing, all-inclusive, nonjudgmental, and unconditional communicates by its very existence that "all is welcome here." There is no part, no aspect of our inner life, history, or our pain; there is no shame, fear, or overwhelm that is not valued, included, or embraced.

When we bring compassion and deep empathic listening to this suffering, we wake up and see it. When we bring our heart to suffering and listen to ourselves, everyone around us feels safer and more secure because we are no longer acting from protection and defensiveness. We communicate energetically—"I will not harm you, I see you, and I am making room for you"—through our voice, our listening, and our actions. Constriction relaxes, and what is released is love and trust. We discover that which is precious—the deep longing that resides at the heart of every moment of pain and suffering. We find the hope and the trust that reside there. What is revealed is beauty that is always precious, that is always there.

*The Fifth Core Principle*

The fifth principle is that when life energy is liberated from these constrictions over and over again and we are in touch with the life force as it authentically lives in us, we start to feel the energy of our longings, and we start to experience release and relief. There is the beauty of acceptance in our pain. At the heart of our loneliness is the yearning to belong. There is the longing to finally be seen and loved unconditionally, regardless of the mistakes we've made. When the longing for unconditional love is released, even in small moments, it becomes available for us to inhabit, embody, and live. When this beauty is revealed through compassion, what is also revealed is the natural movement of this precious life energy to express itself as contribution, creativity, love . . . as life. It naturally seeks creative expression, to live in joy, love, and service. It moves out to live in a flow of life itself.

---

These five core principles of Living Compassion are rather simple, but they have profound implications. Living Compassion invites us—calls us—to claim this life force, to sense it, to feel it, to surrender to it, to live it, to choose it.

I choose to live with passion, and I choose to live with compassion. These are the two streams that orient my whole life, moment by moment: I live with the aliveness of the life force, with the passion of it; and when passion is not fully there, I bring compassion to my experience. This is the foundation of Living Compassion, which I address more fully in chapter 2.

## THE UNFOLDING OF ESSENTIAL BEING THROUGH OUR NEEDS

There is a process I call "unfolding." If something is enfolded, it is covered up, not obvious or readily available. However, *un*folding reveals more and more of what is there. I'd like to elaborate on this using "The Unfolding of Essence, " a diagram I created.

This diagram demonstrates the process of "unfolding." The oval at the top of the diagram represents our essential Being: our essence, our spirit, and our true nature. Next, represented by the sun, our essence unfolds or reveals the *qualities* of our Being. These qualities are inherent to the self. They are already present and whole. These natural qualities of our Being reveal themselves as the longings of our heart, and we refer to these longings as our needs or values.

### THE UNFOLDING OF ESSENCE

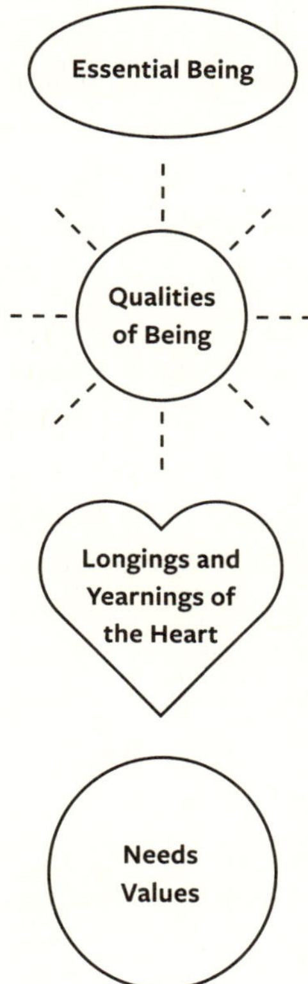


There is a basic life current or impulse resonating in and through us as a yearning of the heart. This current and yearning manifest as human needs.

One of the primary qualities I see as innate to our Being is the quality of love. We are inherently loving; it is our nature. We are inherently compassionate; it is our nature. Another quality of our nature is that we are absolutely free, unbounded, and unperturbed by any kind of limitation. There are a number of other qualities that are inherent to our essential Being, and one of life's challenges is that we are not always able to connect to these qualities.

There are many words that describe the core of who we are: our *essence*, our *essential Being*, and our *true self.* This core is where all the qualities of our essential Being—such as innocence, creativity, aliveness, and love—reside. Whenever we are in touch with ourselves, we experience those qualities as felt, embodied energies that are unmistakably who we are. This is the part of ourselves that we want to experience in fullness; it is what we yearn for in ourselves and in our relationships. When we contact another person authentically and experience a real connection of mutual caring, understanding, seeing, and being seen, it is this—our essential Being—that we are expressing from and what we are contacting in the other person.

The heart shape at the center of the diagram represents the longings of the heart, the qualities that we yearn for. If we long for support in relationships, this felt sense is already alive in our heart. I use the words *longing* and *yearning* to describe the vibration of my Being. If I feel a longing for love or for belonging or to be seen, these tell me that my Being is communicating to me through my heart. It is an energy that awakens me to what matters to me.

Our longings and yearnings of the heart unfold as our needs and values, represented in the circle at the bottom of the diagram. The specificity of how our longings manifest in our lives and relationships is the life current moving through us.

The categories in the diagram are not strictly divided but, for me, they live as delicate distinctions. It's not the words that are important. What is important is the space within, which we are experiencing and living.

The beautiful thing I see about NVC is that it is a way for journeying into deep authenticity. In our essence, we are beings that are alive, and we are in a life flow. We are in a kind of a current, like an electrical current (although this life current is much bigger and deeper), that is a manifestation of our essential Being. It is our life moving through love. Most of us have not been able to access that flow of life, except accidentally. And then we find NVC, touch this current of life, and become aware—"Wow! There's feelings and needs?"

In that moment when we are actually able to express our feelings and needs and are truly heard, it is like dipping into that river of life. But somehow, it doesn't last. We dip into the river of life and we want more. So we go to NVC practice groups and workshops and read books because we want more of that river of life, more of that ability to offer spacious acceptance to someone else, more of being heard and enriched. And we pick up books like this one.

Let's do more than temporarily dip into that river of life. See if you can relax into and allow that flow, seeing and deepening its flow within. The more we practice dipping into it, the more we can live in that energy and flow. For me, this is the practice of Living Compassion that lies at the heart of NVC.

## LIVING FROM A NEEDS-BASED ORIENTATION

One of the things that is important to me when I am sharing anything around Nonviolent Communication is having a kind of flexibility around the words and terms that are used to refer to the energy of needs—something that is both an experience and a consciousness. I use the words *needs* and *values* synonymously. Depending on the context, I may use the words *need* or *value* or even the phrases *what matters to me* or *what is precious to me*. They all refer to the same thing: They are expressions of our essential Being.

For example, if I say, "I have a need for honesty," it's the same thing as saying, "I value honesty." "I have a need for authenticity" is the same thing as "I value authenticity" or "Authenticity matters to me." So, when I am experiencing authenticity or honesty—whether I am receiving it from you or I'm expressing it—that experience is something I feel in an embodied way. It is not just a concept.

When I use any of these words for needs, I am speaking about something that is qualitative, not quantitative. This points to the fundamental distinction in NVC between needs and strategies. A strategy is a specific plan or action that we think will meet our needs. It's often rooted in our learned beliefs and judgments. However, needs are universal human qualities—like love, freedom, or connection—that point to a deeper, more universal experience that does not rely on specific actions or outcomes.

The construct of human needs is important in meaningful and important ways as we develop the capacity to connect with our self and when we are in relationship with other people. Nonviolent Communication helps us tune in to the fact that no matter what another person is expressing or doing, it is always the expression of the life force. This is what is beautiful and powerful about the principle of nonviolence through our communication.

If at any moment I connect with a longing in my heart, that longing is a vibration of something that is *already* whole and present. It is not something that is in the future as an outcome. For example, if I want to be in an intimate relationship and to be close to someone, because I don't have that in my life, I wouldn't say "I long for an intimate relationship." I would say, "I long for intimacy." The form this might take—the strategy, the action I choose to meet the need for intimacy—might be to have a specific person share a period of my time or my life with me.

Whenever we express ourselves authentically, the challenge can be to stay self-connected while speaking. My understanding of why this challenge arises is that authenticity requires a deeper, felt sense of vulnerability that is often unfamiliar. We aren't trained or conditioned in how to give expression to our vulnerability, so that's a capacity that we can develop over time. When this challenge occurs, I suggest suspending the desire to speak and, instead, just dwelling in the energy that is present, feeling it without speaking. As we dwell in the energy of vulnerable authenticity, we begin to trust it more. Our minds have been conditioned to describe the experience and then to express that description rather than allowing the experience itself to find the words. I suggest asking yourself, "Can I allow my experience to find the words?" It doesn't matter what the words are . . . sometimes what comes is just a sound. Trust the authentic self and allow it to express, however it wants to come out.

## EXPRESSING OURSELVES IN THE FLOW OF LIFE

One of the important elements of living through and from ourselves and our needs is that this is something that is felt. So, when we get in touch with the quality of a value, need, or longing, we experience that quality in and through our body. It is an energetic quality. When the need or longing is felt in this way, it is experienced much more fully. When we are in the flow of life, we experience needs as a life force. A more expansive sense of being in a flow of life that moves through our essential Being is accessed through the heart's longings. This is the emergence of the true nature of who we are as human beings. Living a need or quality means our entire consciousness and actions inhabit it. When we are in those moments, then there is a flow.

Experiencing our needs is the doorway to accessing spirituality in life and sharing our Being in relationships. Needs are an aspect or an expression of the Divine as it lives in us. They arise from life and express the requisites necessary to fulfill and nurture life itself. We experience the energy or the beauty of a need—which are synonymous—when we are in contact with the qualities of its energy: We name these as love, compassion, or any of our other longings. When we touch our needs, we feel their energy and experience their fullness. This opens the doorway to something more fundamental, more core.

The notion of needs being the doorway to our essential Being is central to the spirituality of NVC. My intention is to live in this energy of the beauty in needs as much as I can. When we are living in and acknowledging the energy of this essential Being from which our needs are unfolding, we are truly in the flow of life; whether the need is met or unmet does not affect its energy. When a need is not met, we may be sad and mourn, but we are in touch with the energy of our essential Being as we mourn and not oriented toward the loss of this or that outcome in life. I address mourning and celebration more fully in chapter 6. To relate to our needs this way is transformational—for ourselves and our relationships—because healing takes place as a natural unfolding when embodying the fullness of life in the energy of our needs. This is the practice of Living Compassion.

## HOW THE ENERGIES OF LONGING AND LACK AFFECT COMMUNICATION

Often people use the word *longing* when what they mean is *seeking*. There is an important distinction between longing and seeking, and it is a matter of orientation. Longing resides in the heart as an orientation toward the fullness of any quality or need that is *already* present. We are already whole as beings. We are not lacking anything. When we seek something, this implies a deficiency or a lack; we're not experiencing something that we want to experience. For example, if we don't experience being seen or understood, or if there is another unfulfilled need, we might relate to it as lacking the need we've identified rather than valuing the beauty and essential Being inherent within that need. It is this experience of lack that gives rise to seeking. In chapter 4 I will show how a lack orientation arises from the functioning of the thinking mind when it's in a separated state, when the mind's deep tendency is to seek outside itself and project into the future. It is outcome-oriented.

One of the reasons this orientation toward having a specific outcome can be limiting is that when we are expressing a need from the energy of lack or deficiency (whether spoken or not), we are communicating that something is wrong, that we're missing something. This usually means we are attached to an outcome in some way. An orientation of lack also makes it difficult to connect with the other person's needs and requests. A verbal or energetic attachment to an outcome is communicated to the other person with the energy of "I have to have it" and a sense of urgency that comes across as a demand, even if the words are perfectly expressed according to the NVC model. As a result, when we are coming from an orientation of lack, it's almost inevitable that whatever we are expressing communicates a degree of what I call "suffering." When we make a request from a place of lack, we are experiencing some pain within that is calling for a particular kind of attention: compassion.

The words *yearning* and *longing*, in contrast, are vibrations of the heart. Let me give you an example: How do I know that I enjoy intimacy and love? Certainly I enjoy those qualities in real life, in the relationship spaces. But I also know and experience that these qualities are already within me: the quality of love, the quality of intimacy, the quality of beauty. It is the beauty within me that recognizes the beauty outside. It's the love that is already in me that recognizes the love in the relational space. When I touch that internal quality of love, it becomes an energy, a living impulse, that moves me toward love in my relationships. It's as though the heart is the organ of my consciousness. I want to embody my heart consciousness.

Another example of a need in the dimension of relationship is the quality of belonging. If I am connecting with that energy, what I am in touch with is a space where not only I exist but we all exist as a group. This means that when I enter into my heart, you are there, too. There is a quality of belonging in that space in which you and I already are. This may not necessarily be manifest in life, but it is manifest in that place where we exist together already. This is the living reality I get in touch with, that shows up as the longing for something beautiful.

If I am experiencing something missing, it's because of my trauma and conditioning that orient me toward lack. But when I'm experiencing something painful, I can change my orientation. Instead of the pain pointing me toward lack, I can experience the pain pointing me toward what matters to me, toward what I value.

If I am approaching another person from an orientation of lack—maybe a part of me is experiencing judgment or demand, or I want life "different from the way it is"—then I know this part of me is calling for compassion. I need to be heard more deeply about that pain so I can touch into the beauty that is underlying the need. I don't want to judge myself for experiencing lack or to tell myself that somehow lack is wrong. If I'm in this energy of lack, it means I'm in a kind of suffering pain. I can turn toward the pain and allow it to show me what it is that matters to me.

When I feel a longing, on some level and to some degree there is an experience of lack. But it is the part of me that recognizes the energy of lack that is the longing for what matters to me. It is so beautiful. It vibrates in my heart in relationship to what is already in my life. Longing is reminding me, it is calling to me, and it is saying, "This is what is important. This is what I long for." The vibration is already in my heart, and it brings me forward to the life I want to create.

## HOLDING OUR LONGINGS PASSIONATELY, BUT LIGHTLY

When we say a need has been "unmet," that language can be problematic for people. As I mentioned earlier, saying "I need something" implies I am lacking it. That's not what I mean when I use the word *need*. The way we know that a need is not fulfilled is that we are conscious of it. This means we are conscious of our life force—of what we value.

What I mean by "need" is that there is a vibration of my heart that tells me what matters to me. That vibration of my heart is already full. The spiritual practice of this is to hold my needs, my longings, with passion but to hold the outcome lightly, meaning I'm not grasping it. I'm not attached to the outcome. If I am attached to the outcome, then I'm experiencing lack—I am orientated toward lack. Another way to say this is that what I am experiencing isn't in alignment with my life force. There's a misalignment, a dissonance. I want to be primarily oriented toward the life force in every moment. This is the power of what guides me. Moment by moment, I experience life as dissonance, resonance, dissonance, resonance, fulfillment, unfulfillment. But none of my experience is based on lack. It is based on life, which is inherently full.

My orientation when I communicate needs is absolutely essential. When I say, "I have a need for . . ." or "I have a longing for . . . ," it doesn't mean I am lacking it. It means there is an impulse of my nature that I am tuning in to. There is no lack present. The language of life helps me to communicate this. When I say, "What matters to me is understanding," this doesn't mean I lack understanding. The impulse of understanding wants to emerge, and I want it to do that so that I can live the impulse of understanding with you. I want us to live it together, bringing what can be called the "universal essence" into the interpersonal relationship forum. When I have my primary focus on connecting, by which I mean that I am revealing my authenticity and receiving yours, I am less likely to be attached to a specific need being met. Holding our needs passionately and the outcome lightly is one of the central aspects of living this orientation toward fullness in relationships. We can then meet in the space of mutuality.

## PRACTICES THAT SUPPORT LIVING COMPASSION

Receiving my cancer diagnosis in 2018 was a profound and intense experience. But something happened that was almost miraculous. A pathway opened for me, and immediately I felt (beyond a surface fear) an enormous gratitude for life . . . for what life was and is and continues to offer me. This gratitude was so powerful that it was a theme that lasted throughout my whole experience. At the same time, I was able to open and greet the experience. It wasn't very painful, but there was an intense energy of exhaustion. And I just allowed myself to feel completely tired and exhausted. I don't know how to explain the many dimensions of experiencing that accompanied me through this time except that I am grateful for the practices I've discovered and used in my life—that they were there and available for me to be with myself, to allow myself to feel whatever I felt.

I offer guided meditations and other practices in each chapter of this book to help you cultivate a spiritual practice and support you in experiencing however your life unfolds. These practices have been structured in every way as invitations to inner exploration. Each meditation and practice is based on what I have discovered as maps to our inner landscapes, and they have the potential for deeper connection to this mystery and intelligence that I want to follow. My hope for you is that you trust in your own practice—sense what is valuable for you and trust in that. This is what I do.

As you use these practices, you will grow in the foundational capacity to be with and allow your experience. This capacity is at the heart of all the practices I offer. I recommend first developing the basic capacity to be present by practicing with something that is not too intense, as you are developing the ability to be with higher intensity.

My intention is to engage in these practices in my life all the time. Every moment, I want to remember to feel my self, feel the energy in my life, the life in my body. There's a core principle in all of the practices I offer: *Whatever arises, you allow it, embrace it, and love it, just as it is.* You open to whatever you encounter, allow it to be there, and bring compassion to it.

## MEDITATION

### *Exploring the Energy of Love*

**You might want to record the following meditation first and then play it to guide you. Invite yourself to spend time with and notice whatever is present after each question or reflection.**

---

Let's begin.

I invite you to close your eyes and bring into your awareness someone who you love, someone you deeply care about, who you highly regard. Vividly imagine this person. Perhaps imagine being with this person, exchanging words, sharing energy.

As you are imagining this person, bringing them into your heart, just allow yourself to feel the energies and the feelings that arise as you hold this person in your awareness.

Can you feel the emotions that are connected to this energy of love and deep care?

Do you notice your body and how your body vibrates . . . the sensations that your body feels in the quality and energy of love or care or regard?

If anything else arises, just allow that. If something that is unpleasant or uncomfortable or painful arises, just notice and allow that.

Notice if love is taking other shapes. Maybe it takes the form of support. Maybe it takes the form of belonging or beauty. Or maybe it takes the form of other qualities connected to this care, this love that you have.

Notice if there's something in your mind. Maybe there's some thinking . . . thoughts or a story that is arising in your mind as you are invited into this practice. If this happens, just observe it.

And as best you are able, stay connected to feeling this quality, this energy of love or care and, if you can, just slowly remove the other person from this experience. Gently relax your focus on the person and allow yourself to feel just the love itself. Feel it in your body. See if you can breathe with it . . . flow with it.

Although this love came alive with this other person, is it possible to feel the energy of the love just by itself?

Allow yourself to keep breathing fully.

Embodying this quality of love—which is something of a lens for your heart—I invite you to expand your view beyond this initial person to other people. Can you see others through this energy of love?

Now, can you see your community . . . your country . . . all human beings with this energy?

Staying as connected with this energy as you can, allow yourself to dwell in the present moment . . . breathing . . .

And now slowly bring your awareness back to your outer environment as you conclude this meditation.

You may wish to journal from your experience.

**JOURNAL**

## *Expressing the Energy of the Heart*

**This practice can be done alone by journaling or by sharing aloud with someone else. If you are doing this practice alone, you might want to record the invitations first and then play your recording, pausing it to receive and then respond to each question or reflection.**

**If you are doing this practice with another person (the practices offered in this book will refer to this person as your "partner"), they can offer the invitations and then wait as a silent witness while you share your responses aloud.**

**Don't rush through this practice. Take the time you need to connect with each invitation so you can fully receive it. Connect to what's alive and then share (and perhaps write down) what arises.**

---

Let's begin.

I invite you to bring your attention to your body and to your breath. Relax and breathe.

Think of something you have wanted to say to someone but that you have not said. What you want to say doesn't have to be painful or even about an unmet need. It can be about anything you've wanted to express but haven't yet said.

Write down (or tell your partner) what you could say in a way that you believe would have the best chance of being heard. Keep this brief. Rather than going into detail, just choose the essentials you want to communicate.

Now silently reflect on the value, need, or longing that underlies your desire to express this.

When you are ready, write down (or share with your partner) what you have discovered, using one word or a short phrase.

Remember a time when this value, need, or longing was present and it was met. Allow yourself to connect to what it felt like, to experience the energy that was present in you when the need was met back then.

This is more than a mental exercise. It's a memory of the embodied experience of this need that was fulfilled. Remembering is a way to support your connection with the fullness of this need in the present moment, even though it happened in the past. Notice what is alive in you at this moment.

Write down (or share with your partner) your bodily experience of this value, need, or longing in its fullness.

Now, from this place of dwelling in the fullness of the need, write down (or say out loud to your partner) what you could say to this other person who you've wanted to express to but have not. Don't worry about the words; instead, allow the energy of your heart to speak for you.

When you have completed your sharing, if you are practicing with a partner, you can switch roles.

---

Compassionate presence allows the knotted form we feel as constriction to unfold. We do not make it unfold. It unfolds naturally because that is the wisdom of life itself. Healing happens in the presence of love. It is the nature of life unfolding.

CHAPTER TWO

# Following Aliveness

> I have learned that human beings are not searching for philosophies, even though it may seem that way sometimes. We are searching for something we can trust. And when we find ourselves in the midst of change, the philosophies are like a broken crutch. They do not hold us up. What supports us is a force, an energy, a vortex of love that expresses through us as warmth, creativity, service, and compassion.[1]
>
> The journey Home is not an ideological experience. It takes place in the heart, in the great stream of feelings which flow through us. Our return to truth is a return to simplicity and not to cosmic information.[2]
>
> —STEPHEN SCHWARTZ

As you'll remember from the previous chapter, I conceptualize living into the principles of Nonviolent Communication as a twofold spiritual life practice that I call Living Compassion. Every moment in my life, my intention is to live in the *passion* of my life energy and my life force. And at every moment when my life force is obstructed, I want to bring *compassion* to it.

I see passion and compassion as two primary and encompassing processes in life, and they are integrated, intermingled, and interwoven with one another like two streams. They both have a primary orientation toward the already present fullness within us. The orientation of these processes is different from our learned orientation toward lack, which I explored in the previous chapter.

The first stream of my life practice is that I intend to live in this fullness of life energy, to embody what I care about, to live the passion and energy of my needs. I want to experience this passion moment by moment, in the flow of life that changes, varies, and comes and goes. I want to live according to this intention and this energy. I want to live with the qualities of presence, authenticity, and freedom; and I want to live this in my relationships.

Inevitably I will experience moments when the flow of the life stream is blocked; moments when I am not in its flow. When I am not in the flow, it is usually because of a conscious or an unconscious reaction to something someone said or some other life event. This is when I bring in the second stream of my life practice. When I'm in a reaction—contracted, judging, or disconnected—then my intention is to bring that second stream of compassion to these parts of myself and my experiencing.

The obstruction of the life force is the result of our conditioning and our trauma. It manifests as judgments and the reactive experiences of fear, anger, overwhelm, and violence of all forms. In relating to these obstructions, we've learned to judge and make an enemy of these parts of ourselves, stuck in the orientation of problems and lack. The compassion stream of the twofold life practice helps us meet and welcome these obstructions with curiosity, openness, care, and warmth. Through my life practice, I know that compassion sees all obstructions as life longing for fulfillment. When I follow this path, I experience the energy of compassion restoring wholeness and reconnecting me to the underlying beauty of life. This is what it means to practice Living Compassion.

The compassion stream is akin to one of the first principles of Nonviolent Communication. I remember Marshall Rosenberg sharing that all violence—whether physical, emotional, or psychological—is a tragic expression of needs. A different way of conveying the same principle is that every expression we make, even one full of judgment, has at its heart nothing other than life reaching for life. When we can stay in compassion for those who are doing violence and those who are receiving it—because both are suffering—this, for me, is prayer.

What I love about this practice is that it isn't complex. It is not necessarily easy to do, but it's a simple practice. I don't need to be analytical about life. I develop and cultivate passion, the energy of my needs, or compassion when I'm experiencing judgment, suffering, or any other contracted experience. My orientation is always toward the flow of life.

## FINDING THE "YES" IN RELATIONSHIP TO LIFE

There are certain principles I want to remember in my spiritual practice. What matters to me, what I truly long for, is always a "yes" in relationship to life. I want to find the "yes" behind any inner "no" that I experience. For me, a "no" points to what is wrong or what is missing. "No" is an expression of lack rather than of fullness of the life force. It might take a while for me to explore and transform the nature of this "no," and maybe in the process, some conditioned thought will be revealed. However, I'm not trying to find the conditioned thought or trauma. I simply want to open my awareness to see what's revealed when I listen to the energy of the "no." What is this part of me saying? What is this part feeling? What is it scared of? And behind that, what is the "yes?"

When I am connected to the "yes," I am connected to life. A primary focus of this teaching is the development, growth, and cultivation of a foundational embodied consciousness of life and an energetic connection with the life impulse we call human needs. This life impulse shows up in me as "I value belonging," or "I long for understanding," or "What matters to me is being seen," or "I want freedom." These are all different expressions of how the life force shows up as "yes" in me. I always receive any of these as a "yes" and as being connected with life.

The fundamental life force that contains everything is love. It takes the different shapes of all the other qualities: love in the form of support, love in the form of consideration, love in all forms and qualities of our needs. The life force also takes the shape of freedom: my power to choose, moment by moment, whatever it is that I am choosing. I can put my attention on lack (such as habitual, reactive thinking) and the orientation toward "no," or I can put my attention on the flow of life (an inner bodily connection to what is alive in the moment) and the orientation toward "yes."

These practices are not always easy, but they always have a clear intention. Whatever arises, love it. Whatever arises, allow it. Whatever arises, be with it. Most importantly, whatever arises, hold the intention to be aware and sensitive to that inner life, to that inner flow of energy and feeling. This is the guiding intentionality of my twofold, spiritual life practice of passion and compassion. In every moment of life, I want to be fully present. I want to live in my needs and my values. I want to express them. I want to regard other people with the awareness that these people matter to me. This is one of the primary capacities I develop in the work of Living Compassion.

In its initial stages, this orientation toward life can be seen as a conceptual framework and used as a guide, as something to remember. Even if I don't experience it immediately, I can remember, "Okay, this is what I am experiencing—this difficulty; this problem; this contraction, pain, and suffering. Can I remember to go slowly, to breathe, and to bring a particular quality of awareness to meet it rather than resist it?"

I don't know anybody who never gets triggered. I haven't gotten to this place. However, when I get triggered, I want to find the beauty in it. I want to encompass and welcome the life that is in the energy of that contraction.

In every moment, I want my orientation to be toward life, not toward problems, beliefs that something is wrong, or lack in any form. At those times when I am not experiencing the fullness of life, if my intention is to remember to orient myself toward life, to that which is the already present fullness, then this tuning in becomes my guide, and I don't tend to get so sidetracked.

## A FULLNESS FOCUS

One of the ways I see cultivation of this orientation toward life is when I embody it. I see that with my conscious agency I can focus on and direct my life force. What I call "the energy of the heart" is not just a feeling energy. There's an intelligence to the energy, and I can cultivate my ability to direct this intelligent energy of my Being or my heart in very specific ways. One of the specific ways I cultivate this ability is when I bring my intention, and therefore my energy, to distinguishing between what I observe and what I *think* about what I observe—my evaluations, my stories, and my judgments. This directing of my consciousness is one way I conceptualize living NVC.

We are continually putting our attention on something in ourselves, in our inner awareness and inner experience. At the same time, we are focusing on outer experiencing: in our relationships and in life. If meditation is directing attention, you can say that we are always meditating on something. The question is, On what are we meditating? Where is our attention? What is the quality of our attention?

Implied in these questions is that if we're not meditating on something focused, directed, conscious, and present, then we are meditating on the relatively unconscious habituation that can be seen as being safe but limiting. Our attention is focused on some form of habitual, relatively unconscious thinking and acting.

On the other hand, we can choose to have a conscious, deliberate intention to focus our attention on present-moment aliveness and authenticity. The beautiful thing I see about the work of Living Compassion is that it is a map for journeying into presence and deep authenticity. In our essence, we are beings who are living in a life flow. We are in a current, like an electrical current, although this life current is deeper and subtler. This current of life is a manifestation of our Beingness. It is our life moving through love.

## STAYING IN THE FLOW OF LIFE

Nonviolent Communication cultivates discernment that supports the development of many important skills and consciousness that helps us to be more aware and able to live in the flow of life. I encourage practice with them all, and I will elaborate on some.

One important skill to develop is the ability to distinguish between what we are observing and what we are thinking in evaluative and judgmental terms. When I can differentiate my judgments from my observations, I am then freed to enter into a relative openness and vulnerability. Being open and vulnerable is another way of saying, "I am in an undefended state with respect to what I am experiencing." If I am in a defended and protected state, this means that, to some degree, I am in my patterns of judging and evaluating.

My experience is no longer mediated by my thinking, my judgments, and my evaluations when I am open and vulnerable in a direct relationship to a stimulus or observation. In this way, NVC helps me cultivate openness. I can go directly to my heart. In relationship to what others may say, my awareness of needs guides me to ask myself, "What matters to me? What am I needing in relation to this?" Further steps take me into the relationship space, where we invite each other into a mutual experience. I show up, you show up; I express what matters to me, and I hear what matters to you. Out of this space, we can move forward into collaborative action, where we meet each other in our requests.

A basic principle of NVC is that people are always and only expressing the life in them. However, sometimes they do not do this in a clear way. For many people who are new to NVC (and even people who have been around NVC for a while), attempting to connect an experience to a need is often head-centered. They connect to what the word *need* means rather than to their body's intelligence, making the shift from their head to their heart.

We can think about what our needs and values are, and in this way, needs can make some sort of logical sense. But when, instead, we stay with our sensations, it can be like walking across a threshold into a different possibility. This is a distinction I find so important. By remaining open and waiting in this openness, something much larger and more encompassing can emerge that is beyond the mind. One of the reasons I've developed Living Compassion practices is to help people connect to the embodiment of need energy rather than to just the word that describes it.

## CONNECTING FEELINGS—EVEN ANGER—TO NEEDS

Another important capacity developed by NVC is the ability to experience authentic feelings and then connect with our needs and longings so that we can embody and communicate them. One of the fundamental steps in working with the complexity of feelings is to acknowledge that we are feeling something, that something is going on inside us. This requires self-honesty, even if we can't name what we're feeling.

The capacity to feel and acknowledge what we are feeling is such an important element of being self-connected and self-aware. And we must be able to notice what we are feeling to convey to another person the degree of authenticity we are living.

"Feelings" and "emotions" are two words that are often used interchangeably, but they can also be used differently. If we have a sensation, our experience of that sensation can be that we are feeling something. If there's an emotional feeling, then it's a different kind of experience. Both are feelings: either an emotional feeling or a physical feeling, a sensation. I don't think there's an absolute definition for the word *feeling*; it depends on who is speaking and how they are defining it. I like to qualify what I am describing in this way: "I'm having an emotional feeling," meaning I am experiencing certain emotions such as warmth, joy, happiness, relief. I describe a feeling of energetic flow in my body as a physical sensation or a felt sense. My experience of this energy is that "I am feeling it," but what I am experiencing is not an emotional feeling.

There is a distinction between what I call "reactive feelings" and more heart-connected feelings, which I call "nonreactive" or undefended, vulnerable feelings. For example, it might be that underneath an experience of anger, I am feeling scared. The anger is a way to protect myself from the more vulnerable feeling of fear. It also might be that my fear has a story that projects into the future and predicts that something is going to happen. To see a thought for what it is and not allow ourselves to fuse into it or identify it as the actual truth is extremely important. Recognizing that a thought such as "I am unworthy" is a belief, a story I'm telling myself and I believe in, might take layers and layers of unfolding. I call a number of defended feelings "whole experiences" because they include thinking or creating a story and are therefore more than emotions. I see anger as a valid, authentic experience, but it is reactive in that it usually carries within it some sort of judgment or enemy image or projection onto the other person or myself.

So, the evaluative thought or story in that judgment is not a feeling, yet it is a component of the "whole experience" we call anger. I want to recognize that anger is authentic and that there are two different ways of experiencing it. One way can be expressed as, "I am angry because something matters to me, and it is that which matters to me that I'm needing and valuing." I want to remember that anger is about my needs. If I don't remember this, then I'll end up in the other way, which is one of blame and judgment and enemy images whose expression is "I'm angry because of *you*!" This kind of reactive thinking almost always goes with anger. When I'm angry, I'm going to be in my head, judging the other person. When I am in that state, who's suffering? They aren't; I am.

Marshall Rosenberg pointed out that anger tells us two things. One is that we are going into our heads, where we are creating enemy images that are full of evaluations and judgments. The other is that there are needs we are not in touch with. To help us be present with the intensity of anger, to create some inner space, and ultimately to transform anger, we can acknowledge and name our judgments and enemy images and then connect to our needs, to the energy of what matters to us. Transformation may not come easily, but at least this process provides a map to navigate the inner territory of our anger.

It can be challenging being with the energy of someone who is expressing their anger in front of us. They are angry about something and expressing what's important to them. It takes quite a focus to connect to what matters to them when we're being stimulated by their anger. Some deep conditioning in us tells us, "It's dangerous! I don't want to be around it. I get scared when someone is angry." The more we engage in our inner work, when this fear has been stimulated, the more we are able to be increasingly present to the person when they express anger in front of us. It depends on many things. Do I have the space to pause? Can I listen to the person's anger and hear what they are angry about? Can I let them know that I hear what they are angry about—that something matters to them—and reflect even just that?

The important skill of transforming our own anger and approaching the anger of others is remembering that there is always an orientation toward life that we can choose. If we are angry, it is because something matters. If we are angry, can we transform our anger and own or embrace the passion behind it? Then can we express openly, vulnerably, and tenderly what it is that matters to us? Otherwise what we are likely to communicate is our judgments, and these will create more defensiveness.

Living Compassion invites awareness underneath the anger and fear so that we can touch into the more vulnerable parts of our experience and reside in our essential Being.

## NEEDS ARE AN EXPRESSION OF ESSENTIAL BEING

As we explored in the previous chapter, needs are an aspect or an expression of the energy of life. They arise from life, expressing the requisites of life necessary to sustain itself. We experience the beauty of a need when we are in contact with the quality of its energy. This reaching to contact the energy of the need is an aspect of wanting to nurture and extend life. Holding our awareness on living from this divine life impulse is the intention to nurture and extend the life that is expressed within the energy of every essential living need.

There are two meanings to the phrase *meet our needs*. One meaning is to request something of people, giving them the opportunity to do something to contribute to our well-being. This is a function of action. I (or someone else) will use a strategy—take an action—to fulfill a need.

Another way to "meet" a need is to get acquainted with how this need lives in us as an expression of our essence. When we do this, when we touch that need, we are touched by life, and we live the quality of this need in our very Being. This is a function of attention. By using our attention, we can become aware of our needs as they live in us. We become acquainted with our needs and, by embracing them, we fully and energetically experience the quality of our needs without regard to their fulfillment.

Developing the ability to focus our attention on and cultivate the intention to connect to the life energy within our needs is one of the most important abilities we develop with Nonviolent Communication. It is the embodied spirituality of NVC. In touch with our essence, we follow the longing, the yearning, to experience this quality of the ecstatic flow of life. When we do this, we are in touch with the need in an embodied way. We experience its qualities, its essence, how it feels when that need is met. We experience this "met-ness" in our body, our emotions, and our very Being.

## MEDITATION

### *Connecting with Wholeness*

**Every need has a quality of wholeness in it. Developing a familiarity with this wholeness is a kind of meditation. By practicing this, we begin to live from the core of these qualities.**

**In the following meditation and journaling practice, I ask you to connect to a personal relationship because I think it can be easier to relate to acceptance and trust in interpersonal relationships.**

**The intention of this meditation is to connect to the fullness of life energy through your heart. Although this meditation focuses on the need for acceptance, and the following journaling prompts focus on the need for trust, these practices can be applied to any need.**

**You might want to record the meditation first, and then as you play it to guide you, spend time with and notice whatever is present after each question or reflection.**

---

Let's begin.

I'd like to invite you to become centered, however you do that. You might want to start by noticing your breath . . . then close your eyes and bring your attention to your body.

Feel the sense of awareness in you and around you. As you do this, breathe and notice if you can relax more. This is not a passive relaxation; it's a very alert form of relaxation.

Connect with your reason for being here, your intention for taking time to do this meditation. You also tune in to the significance, the importance of you being here, present.

Feel your body, solid, sitting in the seat.

Now, take a few minutes to remember a time when you experienced acceptance (or any other need you'd prefer to explore), perhaps in relation to another person. You might express this to yourself as "My need for acceptance was met fully" or "I had the experience of being fully accepted by another person."

Remember this experience as vividly as you can. You can even see, visualize, or remember words that were said. Remembering often helps to connect to the energy of the need you are exploring. The most important part of this practice is to feel the embodiment of the specific quality of acceptance.

Now, bring your memory into the present moment. As you remember, do you feel that quality, the actual experience of the need for acceptance being met? In this quality, is there a sort of recognition that all of you is welcomed and accepted? Take a moment to dwell in this feeling, in this energy of a real experience you had.

Allow yourself to simply feel that energy of acceptance. Feel it in your body. Notice the emotional feelings that come with this energy. Notice whatever else arises in this practice. Just allow it.

There may be some tenderness. There may be some painful feelings. Just allow whatever is there to be there. Allow yourself to breathe.

Maybe another quality comes into your consciousness, and you can name it. Is there a quality of care? Perhaps a feeling of warmth? Simply allow yourself to dwell and bathe in this energy in your body.

Whether your experience is of another person accepting you or you are remembering the experience of extending acceptance toward another person, just stay with it and become familiar with this felt experience.

As you slowly bring your attention back, take another moment—with your eyes closed or open—to continue the practice a little bit longer.

Can you imagine speaking from this energy?

Can you imagine speaking to a person, to someone you care about, to someone for whom acceptance matters both ways—giving and receiving?

Do you sense an openness? Perhaps a tenderness, a vulnerability as you might reveal yourself to what is very dear to you?

Take a few breaths, shift your energy, and allow the energy you've connected with in this practice to stay in you. You can continue by connecting with the energy of another need now. When you are finished, see if you can bring the energy of these needs into the rest of your day. Or on another occasion, you can do this meditation with a different need by first becoming centered and bringing your awareness into the present moment, noticing your breathing, and then remembering a time when that need was met, repeating the meditation guidance given for "acceptance."

## JOURNAL

## *Exploring the Energy of Trust*

**This practice can be done alone by journaling or by sharing aloud with someone else. If you are doing this practice alone, you might want to record the invitations first, then play your recording, pausing it to receive and then respond to each question or reflection.**

**If you are doing this practice with another person, they can offer the invitations and then wait as a silent witness while you share your responses aloud.**

**Don't rush through this practice. Take the time you need to connect with each invitation, so you can fully receive it. Connect to what's alive, and then write down (or share aloud with your partner) what arises.**

---

Let's begin.

I invite you to bring your attention to your body and to your breath. Relax and breathe.

As you did when connecting with the energy of acceptance in this chapter's meditation, remember an experience, a person, or a relationship in which you experienced, or do experience, trust . . . whatever the word *trust* means to you. Bring this relationship into your mind right now and reflect on it as vividly as possible. Maybe you remember some of the things that were said or done in this relationship.

Now, bring the embodied energy of your memory into the present moment. As you remember, do you feel that quality, the actual experience of trust? Take a moment to notice how you feel, how your body feels, and write down (or share aloud with your partner, if you're comfortable) your experience.

Relax into the energy of trust as you are holding the image of this person.

Perhaps you feel the energy of trust as a longing, as something precious to you, that you long to experience in your relationships.

Notice and write down if other qualities are interwoven with trust. Perhaps you sense care, perhaps peace. Maybe there's a feeling of warmth or joy. Whatever arises with the felt energy of trust, allow yourself to relax into it and feel it in your body.

Sometimes the mind comes in. Just notice what the narrative, evaluative mind is telling you. Maybe it is saying something about this exercise and how you're doing it or how you're not doing it. In my experience, this part of the mind can be quite persistent and can come up at times that I don't always enjoy. If this happens for you, simply allow it to be there and observe it. Continue your journaling and reflection.

Notice and write down if there are other relationships where you long for trust. Maybe this includes the one you brought into this practice today. Put your focus on the longing in your heart for trust (not the lack of it). Notice your longing arises from the fullness of what you deeply value, what is precious, what is dear to you.

Allow yourself to feel and record whatever comes up.

Sometimes sadness comes up because what we long for is not as fully present as we would want.

This feeling, this energy, is full; it's filled with life. It is an impulse that moves us forward in our life, in our relationships.

Just let yourself keep with your breath and allow the energy to move and take different shapes and intensities.

Staying with your breath and slowly coming back into your full space, finish recording any final thoughts. Allow yourself to stay connected to this feeling energy as much as you can.

Memory is a way to help connect to the energy of a need. For example, if I were doing this practice without the memory part, I would say, "Can I connect to the energy of acceptance or trust? What do acceptance or trust feel like when they are being fulfilled for me?" I use these questions to touch the energy within each of these needs.

The important question I ask myself is, "What are the qualities and the energy of my need?" As I sink into this embodied experience of my need, I recognize that this is the energy of my heart. This is life energy. It is life speaking to me and through me, and it is the same life energy I am receiving from others.

---

What serves us is a deep intuitive trusting and plunging into our own experience of intending to be present with ourselves, with another, in a bodily felt, heart-centered presence.

CHAPTER THREE

# Transforming Suffering

When your emotional world is alive, it can feel as if you must act urgently to bring relief to the fire within. A familiar sense of overwhelm is present. The panic has returned.

In these moments, slow way down. Rest your tired mind and your achy heart. Descend out of the vivid narrative and into the earthy, muddy ground of your body. Surround the sacred material with your presence and offer safe passage to the temporary, wavelike intensity that is washing through. It is not an enemy but a harbinger of integration.

The inner landscape is being painted by the abandoned ones of your holy nervous system, seeking the light of cohesion and wholeness. Dare to consider that nothing has gone wrong and that you have not failed. It is only the light of the path, come in a form the mind may never understand. Trust in the holding field of your body.

The beloved is coming to know herself, through the vastness of somatic revelation. She is the artist and your heart her canvas. Your body and your senses are her poetic offering to a weary world.

—MATT LICATA[3]

MATT LICATA'S WORDS are a beautiful, poetic description of a journey into the interior landscape of our inner experience. They contain much of the essence of embodied self-compassion. What is self-compassion? It is a practice that helps us to recognize the blocks or obstructions to the flow of our life energy, restore that flow, and change our relationship to pain. The practice of self-compassion is particularly important when we encounter those difficult situations and we don't know how to recover ourselves and our center.

In the previous chapters, I described the nature of Living Compassion, and I introduced my two primary, encompassing, life-oriented processes. They are two streams of focus—two streams of aliveness, consciousness, and energy. One focus is flowing with the life force and embodying the energy of my *passion* of that which I care about. The other focus is the practice of *compassion*, meeting and welcoming with curiosity, openness, care, and warmth anything that obstructs this life force.

Passion is the life force, the life energy emanating from that which already is—the fundamental unity of life. With passion, my intention is to embody, live, and express the authenticity of my Being. I want to dwell in the energy of my heart and a deeply felt sense of what really matters to me. I value truth, honesty, compassion, and nonviolence. I value holding my own needs and my own mattering fully and equally, with myself and with other people. The values I hold in my heart show up in many different ways. One way to describe them is that they are what I am passionate about or what I deeply care about.

The first stream of my spiritual life practice is living into and manifesting my passion in what I care about, so I can live with as much fullness and energy as possible. It can be described as along an "in the flow of life" spectrum. I don't know that I am ever fully in this flow with life or that I am ever fully out of it. But when I am living in the energy of my needs, in the energy of my heart, I experience this as a flow. I experience a strength in my energy and a clarity in my mind.

When I am not in this flow—when I encounter a life event that is difficult to experience—and I examine my own internal response in relation to it, the internal characteristic of this experience is one of blocking the flow. I experience an energetic block on a physical level. The purpose of the second stream of my spiritual life practice is to establish and cultivate a relationship of compassion with my pain, in whatever form I am experiencing it. Doing this entails focusing my attention and bringing a particular quality of awareness to be with this contracted constellation of pain.

## MEETING PAIN WITH AN OPEN HEART

I've found that noticing what I am doing in relation to pain, particularly if I am projecting or my reaction comes from a defensive or protective part of me, is an essential part of taking ownership of my inner experience. Taking ownership can mean that when I feel pain in relation to a stimulus, I notice there is a thought in me and that this thought is a story. I may not say this thought to the person. I would prefer to acknowledge it first with myself—inwardly, interiorly—before I speak.

Taking ownership is the recognition and the conscious acknowledgment that what is arising is coming out of my own interior space, my own system, and my own history. An important support in loosening my fusion with my reaction is to name whatever I can notice in my awareness. By naming it, I might be able to feel it. Can I feel the sensation without bouncing off its energy by either attacking or withdrawing?

For example, let's imagine I am having a conversation with someone and I say something that is important to me, but the response I get tells me that my intention has not been received. I then interpret the other person's response as an evaluation of what I said. I'm evaluating their evaluation. When I receive their response in this way, I may first feel frustrated or angry. My mind says, "Why aren't they getting what I said? I thought I was being pretty clear."

If I can take time to breathe, to allow whatever is arising in me, and to recognize and stay with my thoughts, I find that underneath this reaction there is a sense of tenderness that I feel. I notice a part of me that feels scared. Can I sit with my sadness? Can I sit with the fear?

Almost always, this part of me has a legacy of the pain that the little boy in me felt when he wasn't seen or heard. At the heart of that pain there is a longing to be seen, accepted, and underneath that, to be valued. When I am able to feel this, I may touch the natural pain of grief and this links me to what really matters to me; I begin to feel the energy of acceptance. Even though the need for acceptance was not met in the original conversation, I can now experience the energy of my longing for acceptance and being seen. It is this energy that restores me.

At the heart of all pain is the beautiful life energy, the preciousness of what was lost in those early moments of trauma in which part of me wasn't seen and wasn't understood. That energy is still there as the potential to be seen and embraced. When I see that part of myself, I cherish it. Every time I let that part be felt, I become more whole.

For me, pain is a form of my life force that points to what matters to me. I call this "natural pain." In this undefended relationship with my pain, I experience the fullness of what I value, not the lack of it.

When I move into vulnerable sadness, I am touched by what is precious and beautiful in my heart. This kind of sadness I describe as "sweet pain." This pain is not constricted; it is tender and relaxed. When I get in touch with pure, openhearted sadness, there is a kind of sinking into it, a relaxing, and a letting go. This sweet and natural pain is absolutely essential to fully living my authenticity. Living with an open heart means living with a broken-open heart. This requires a willingness to feel pain when something I experience isn't in harmony with what I hold dear, as well as a willingness to feel the joy that emerges when there is resonance. When I live with an open heart, pain and joy are equally embraced. This is how I bring the second stream of compassion to my experience of pain.

Unless I am in the place where I hold pain and joy as equal, I know I am resisting life in some way. If I want joy more than pain, then I am resisting being fully present in the fullness of my heart in that moment. I want to remember that encompassing presence has a higher order that embraces both pain and joy. When I arrive in this embracing place, I feel the higher order of presence. It is an experience of Grace.

To be fully present to life, I must be present to all of life's experiences, pain, and joy. When I am inhabiting this state of presence, I am aware that emotional pain can't hurt me and that it is an inner guide that points me to my heart. When I am seated in my heart, nothing can hurt me there.

When I'm experiencing the pain of something that is deeply valued in my life but not fulfilled, I can mourn it or I can suffer with it. When I'm suffering with it, the element that I'm adding is a thought or a story about my experience. It is a felt sense when I am in that moment of pain, which is associated with a story: I am suffering because I am in a cycle of disconnection.

When I am in pain, what matters to me is my relationship to it. If I have a relationship with my pain where it closes me off and puts me into my reactive and judgmental mind, I call this suffering pain rather than natural pain.

Suffering is disconnected from life. It is our thinking that creates our suffering—being caught up in the illusion of whatever we are telling ourselves and believing about the situation and our pain. We suffer when we are separated from our heart and from the authenticity of our needs.

When I am in a suffering state, the nature of my internal experience is contraction. With a physical contraction, I may feel hot, tight, heavy, and sometimes numb (which can be both a physical sensation and an emotional experience). I may feel the contraction of reactive emotions such as fear or anger or any of their variations and modifications. I may also be contracted in my thinking, which then becomes very narrow and focused on polarizations such as right and wrong, good and bad, power over and power under, submission and rebellion. Suffering pain can also restimulate past trauma with all of its associated stories.

What I want is to remember that pain connects me to my life force, to my needs and my values, and I want to remember that I can choose this orientation to life.

If I am experiencing something I care about in connection with a need that was unfulfilled, I often feel a degree of sadness and grief. This is natural pain arising in response to mourning. When I open myself to feel the natural pain arising when something I deeply care about is unfulfilled, mourning always points me toward the beauty of my needs. Mourning is an essential part of a spiritual practice. If I am not in touch with the beauty, then I am not in fullness. This doesn't mean I have to experience fullness, but this awareness is a useful indication for me.

## BRINGING COMPASSION TO OUR EARLY WOUNDING

My intention is to live in the present moment and to compassionately embrace my pain. I recognize that all of my deeper pain comes from my young years, and it shows up when it gets triggered. I particularly want to bring compassion to these young, wounded parts of me. I want to open vulnerably to myself and feel the tenderness within me as much as I can. When I do this, I establish an intimate relationship with that young part of me that did not experience what he needed. There is a beautiful, intimate relationship I can generate with this part of me.

I also want to be watchful and to notice the tendency of this young part to project the inner child's urgency to have needs fulfilled into my adult life and to expect others to meet them. I don't think there's anything "wrong" with doing this, but when I can orient toward my inner young self, I feel this inner tenderness. I no longer have this compelling sense of grasping, desperation, or deficiency.

Sometimes I suggest approaching this young part as I would an innocent child who is scared or hurt. This young, innocent part reacts to difficult situations in life by seeking to protect itself because it sees events and situations as dangerous and possibly hurtful or restrictive, as they may have been in the past.

The way I have learned how to transform this kind of deep pain is by turning that inner child around so I face him. Even if this young, wounded part of me is desperately seeking acceptance from others, I know I am the one he deeply needs acceptance from now. He wants to know he is safe with me and that he matters to me. When I view this part of me as innocent, it awakens compassion, and then the constriction begins to relax. In an environment of inner compassion, healing is possible.

## RELAXING INTO SELF-COMPASSION

The approach to inner compassion carries an intention that is life-centered, not pain-centered. What this means is there is an intention to meet the pain with recognition and compassion. Even though I may not have a direct experience of this intention at the beginning, I recognize that life itself is at the heart of all pain. Remember, at the core of all of our pain are unmet and unfulfilled longings. When we are able to bring a particular quality of awareness to our contracted pain, more internal spaciousness is created.

In the course of life, whenever I encounter another person doing or saying something that I don't enjoy—or I experience any event I don't enjoy—I want to notice that I am being stimulated and recognize when there is a painful contraction, a pulling in, and usually an inability to free myself or restore my wholeness. I want to notice I am cutting myself off, or I have a felt sense of being cut off from a relaxed, present flow of energy. Bodily tension and contraction are components of restricting the flow of my energy that I want to recognize. There is also usually a narrative, a story (which sometimes I may not consciously recognize) that shows up in the form of judgments and evaluations and, sometimes, intellectual analysis.

Often when I am scared or angry, when I experience the reactive emotions of overwhelm or powerlessness, I feel them in my body as tension. The important part of this practice of self-compassion is to recognize and acknowledge my experience of contraction and simply to say to myself, "I'm noticing that my body feels tight in relation to what I just observed. I am sensing an emotion of fear or anger," or whatever the emotion is.

I'm not suggesting you try to relax the tension; that would be a strategy. I'm suggesting that you *bring your attention* to the tension, as it is, without trying to relax it. When we do this, relaxing emerges naturally because the attention creates space. The relaxation, the result, is an emergent, natural process.

Even when I begin this process by scanning my body, there's a recognition that brings with it more internal space between the one who is observing (me) and the observed content of my experience (the tension, emotions, and thoughts). This is the pathway of self-compassion, and it is one of the primary skills that I cultivate in the Living Compassion practice.

## DEVELOPING THE CAPACITY TO BE WITH ALL OF OUR EXPERIENCES

One of the first elements in the practice of self-compassion is pausing and breathing. When I focus my awareness, my breath helps me to slow down so that I can encounter the physiological nuances of the contraction and my automatic thoughts.

Another element in the practice of self-compassion is holding a clear intention to "be with" whatever I am experiencing. I've been conditioned to try to get away from pain. If I'm feeling something painful, my conditioning tells me, "I want to feel better. I want to escape the pain; I want to alleviate it." With a lot of psychological and emotional reactive pain, this process of moving away from pain is counter to self-compassion because it is a way of resisting my experience. In the act of avoiding it, I consciously or unconsciously judge the pain as bad or wrong.

The intention of compassion is completely different from this resistance. Rather than attempting to get away from any pain, suffering, or discomfort, my intention is to allow it just to be there, to let the nature of this experience be present. Although this might sound simple, it can be challenging in practice. Allowing the experience and simply being with it is a learned skill, and when I am able to do this, I can begin to feel an almost immediate relief, even if just a little bit.

Developing my capacity to be with my experience transforms my relationship to the pain. Rather than resisting pain, I begin to allow it to be. I tell myself, "It's okay to feel this," even if a part of me is railing against feeling it and is convinced that it is not okay. When I enter into the experience of resistance, the parts of me I resist become enemies; they become something I am trying to get away from. The spiritual part of my Being, which is compassion, wants to befriend these inner enemies.

I have found it very helpful to identify and relate with the different aspects of my Being. For example, if I'm feeling scared, I want to change the language so that instead of saying, "I'm scared," I want to say, "There's *a part of me* that is scared. There is an energy in my Being that is fearful." Self-compassion embraces all parts of me.

The more I engage in a practice of compassion, the more compassionate awareness becomes strengthened. If the nature and the quality of my experience don't relax as quickly as I expect them to, then the part of my mind that gets impatient might say, "I'm trying this, but it is not working!" One of the most important capacities to develop within myself is patience, which is a form of self-trust. Compassion, awareness, patience, and self-trust are some of the many capacities I develop as I practice inner compassion.

Self-compassion can also be called a form of inner empathy. As my consciousness focuses on these inner parts of myself, I become curious about them. I begin to want to find out more. "What is it that is in the fear?" I may invite the fear to speak to me. "What are you scared of? What is the story in the fear? What am I telling myself about the fear?" As I do this, I open up a space for inner dialogue so I can listen deeply to these parts of myself rather than trying to avoid them. When I try to get past my fears, my reactions, my frustration, my overwhelm . . . what I am doing is pushing them to the margins of my awareness so I won't acknowledge them. Any marginalized parts of me will continue to affect the quality of my experience, even if it appears as though I have escaped them.

Self-compassion can be seen as a form of gathering all of the parts of myself that I've pushed away. Now I invite them and, as I welcome them, I begin to feel a warmth and a tenderness toward these parts of myself. I begin to generate a quality of care for them. As I move through these protective parts of myself, I may feel more vulnerability.

Vulnerability opens the door to feel the mourning or grief underneath the fear and anger, which are more protected states of feeling. Compassion is a process of transforming. As these parts transform, they become softer, they relax, and they become open.

The principle that I return to again and again is that at the very heart of my pain is the quality of life, the quality of beauty, which usually takes the form of unfulfilled needs, unfulfilled longings. Something I invite people to experience is that the beauty of these needs is present, whether or not they are being fulfilled. It's a different experience when needs are not being fulfilled than when they are, but the underlying beauty, for me, is the most important part of the experience.

## TRANSFORMING PAIN

One of the principles of this practice is that it is experientially an embodied awareness and not an intellectual process. The practice is not something I "think about." Teacher and writer Stephen Schwartz explains the difference between these.

> Pain is not healed by ideas. It can never be healed by adjusting our thoughts. Pain can't be solved by conceptual struggles of what is going on. Pain is healed by coming to it directly and attending to it as it is and not as we want it to be. Pain does not leave, it is transformed. The very energy that lies at the base of pain is the energy that we want.[4]

If a person says something to me that my mind receives as a harsh judgment or hurtful, I want to notice that this is a judgment arising in me. Something is said, and I have this painful impact on my body. I feel something not only in my body but also in my emotions. Initially I might feel angry, and I may experience judgment in my mind. The form that the painful, reactive experience takes is modified by the thinking that I have if I'm judging. It has this emotional suffering pain. But when I focus my attention in a welcoming way on the parts of me that are contracted, the "it" I am approaching—that whole reality or constellation of inner experiencing that I call pain—transforms. To "trans-form" means that the formation of the contraction changes.

The essence of the energy of pain is the same, but its shape is transmuted, so to speak.

For example, when I stay with my anger and look underneath it, I may recognize that I'm telling myself that this person is wrong and inconsiderate. As I stay with this recognition, and as I tune in to my heart, I feel hurt as a tender and undefended pain. The pain shows me what I value and what I care about. When I tune in to my value for being considered with care, for being seen and understood, I recognize that these are the values and the energy that are behind the pain and hurt. This deeper exploration then transforms my initial experience of judgment and anger into the energy that I so value. In my vulnerability, and attuned with my heart's longing, that anger may unfold into natural sadness and grief, as well as the need to mourn.

I want to take a moment to clarify the distinction I have between transformation and transcendence, as many people find these confusing. There are a couple of meanings of the word *transcendence*. According to certain spiritual practices, if I transcend, the material I'm transcending is still available in my unconscious as the shadow or the dark side that I repress. I am not particularly interested in that kind of transcendence.

However, there is another process of transformation that allows me to transcend—to differentiate from what I am identified with. If I am identified with my suffering, these constellations of energies that keep me in the reactive state, then I want to bring compassion to my reactive thinking and allow it to transform. In this case, transcendence is actually differentiation. If I transcend my evaluative thinking, then I can reside in the observational mode. I'm more empowered and can allow the transformation of that which I've differentiated from. Eventually this process allows me to connect more to the fullness of what is the heart of the pain that is in my suffering in the first place.

In essence, a spiritual life practice transforms where and how we center our attention and energy. This means reclaiming our power from dependence on the external world: our things, circumstances in our environment, and the opinions of other people. We discover the source of our strength and presence.

The attention and energy of living—our center of gravity—transforms and connects us to our heart and soul. When we transcend, we can live a soul-centered life. We make an inner move from reacting to the exterior reality to abiding in the power and clarity of consciousness. We allow the inner qualities to be a guide to living and engaging in life.

## MEDITATION

### *Compassionately Embracing Our Experience*

**You might want to record the following meditation first and then play it to guide you. Spend time with and notice whatever is present after each question or reflection.**

---

Let's begin.

I'd like to invite you into a guided practice. Let's pause for the moment. Breathe, and slowly allow your inner felt experience, whatever it is . . . just to be . . . just as it is. As we breathe, we create a spaciousness.

If there is any pain, instead of resisting the painful contraction by reacting to a story, interpretations, or any thinking that causes the constriction, allow the breathing to relax the body . . . and allow the space.

Sense that there is room for this inner feeling experience to be. There's nothing wrong or right about this feeling. There is nowhere to go, nothing to fix. You are okay just as you are. You are welcoming instead of resisting the feeling experience.

Feelings are energy flowing through the body as sensory, emotional realities. Life energy is flowing through you. It is not right or wrong, appropriate or inappropriate. Everything you feel is life seeking to flow, just wanting to be. As you allow this, vulnerability may arise.

Notice if you are having a tight, constricting experience the more you do this. If you can open to any constriction, perhaps you can view this vulnerable part of you as a very young part, a very innocent part.

If there is a painful feeling, notice . . . is there a wanting or a quality of longing? Can you feel the longing?

As you feel the longing energy, can you sense this longing is for something that is precious? Perhaps for something that relaxes and is deeply comforting? Perhaps you long for love or for a loving presence in which you can relax and feel safe, knowing you are held with care and tenderness?

As you continue this practice, you can let yourself relax into the flow of your breathing . . . gently allowing this life energy of feeling to flow.

Maybe you even feel the sacredness of this energy. Can you notice that this energy is bigger than you? It is life's energy moving through you like a river. There's a sense of strength and clarity in the presence of this feeling as you relax into it and allow it to gently hold you and encompass you.

There is a deep beauty in this living quality and feeling. You are allowing the beauty to be. You are feeling the energetic quality of this beauty . . . staying with it . . . giving yourself time to feel the energy of what is precious.

Dwelling and resting in the energy of what is precious . . . breathing and extending it to your entire body, to every cell in your body, to each limb, to the tips of your fingers and your toes . . . and beyond . . . let this experience extend into the room you are in . . . and let it expand out into the field . . . touching and imbuing everyone you can see and sense, everyone you can imagine, everyone in the entire world.

I invite you to stay and dwell in this feeling. Relax any thinking about it. You can use this practice regardless of what you are experiencing inside, whether it's painful or not, just allowing whatever it is.

When you are ready, you can open your eyes.

## JOURNAL

### *Integrating Our Inner and Outer Experiences*

Don't rush through this practice. Take the time you need to connect with each invitation so you can fully receive it. Connect to what's alive, and then write down what arises. If you are journaling, leave yourself space after writing down each response to let the words feel received. Be both the speaker and the receiver for your experience.

When we are living a nonresistant, nonjudgmental, compassionate relationship to others, the world, and life, we are integrating our inner and outer experiences.

This practice helps me to remember compassionate awareness: what I call "bringing attention to whatever arises." It is the second stream of the practice of Living Compassion. As we journal through (or share aloud, if doing this with a partner) one phase or step of this practice, it may shift our experience. Then we may move into another experience, but the thoughts and reactive feelings come up again. Whatever arises, we stay with or return to it and be with it. We acknowledge that this is what is arising in this moment.

Although there are a number of steps to the following practice, there is no notion of progressing from one step to the next in the usual way we were conditioned to think. Our mind might say, "Oh, I did this step and this step, so why am I back to an earlier step again?" That could be how our mind evaluates this practice, but that is not how integration works, in my experience.

This is an organic process to help us stay with our aliveness, with its organicity and unpredictability. We stay with life. It may be that this experience is telling us that we need to attend to it more. Maybe we are needing more time, more spaciousness. This is how the process of life works, too. A new and unexpected dimension arises and, if it is real and genuine, we feel it, then we trust it. It confirms in us the mystery of life and our surrender to it. It shows us—it guides us—into these completely unpredictable spaces that are so alive.

If you are doing this practice with another person, they can offer the invitations and then wait as a silent witness while you share aloud your responses in

**each step. Begin by choosing who will speak first and who will receive first (and speak second). If you are the first speaker, start slowly, taking time to connect with your experience at each step before sharing with your partner what comes up in you. If you are the receiver—the empathic witness—be as fully present as you can, receiving the energy in the words that are shared by the speaker. As the receiver, listen in silence or reflect what is shared if the speaker requests reflection. Allow a certain amount of time for one person to move through the entire practice before switching roles.**

---

Choose an outer stimulus in your life and write it down in your journal or share what it is with your partner.

Breathe. As you put your attention on your stimulus, focus your awareness on your body.

Simply be with the experience, whatever it is. Allow it to be, just as it is. Just sit with it. A metaphor I often use is of an inner room, your inner living room, and these parts of the experience are your guests. You sit with them. You don't have to do anything. You don't even have to engage them. Just sit with them.

Notice and identify any thinking, stories, or judgments that arise in your mind. Simply notice them. This is an observing practice. Then write them down or share them aloud with your partner.

Focus on your body's sensations and your feelings. Notice any intensity and pain and allow yourself to be with it to the degree that you can. Notice you are engaging in a relationship with this pain or intensity.

Sense into the feelings and sensations you notice, and inquire, "What is this energy longing for?" Is there a need, a value, or something you long for in this energy? You may sense something, and it may not have words. Or it may have words such as "This energy is longing for love" or "In this energy, I sense that I am wanting cooperation and engagement." Connect to the energy of the longing, whatever it is.

While connecting to the energy, feel it in your body. Dwell in the felt sensing of your need.

Now, write down your inner experience of this event or share it with your partner before you continue.

When you are ready to explore integrating your inner with your outer experience, focus your attention once again on the outer stimulus or event you just explored. Take time to notice that your awareness is now on the outer event.

Now focus your attention back on your inner experience.

Notice your awareness is holding your outer and inner observing at the same time, but you are also holding them each as distinct. There is the outer event . . . and then there is the inner experience.

Now continue to alternate your attention between them. Focus on your inner experience (whatever you are experiencing in this moment), and then shift your focus to the outer event. Move back and forth between the two in this way a few times. Allow yourself to experience whatever emerges from moving back and forth.

As you near the end of this process, notice if there is a request you have of yourself as you are connected to this energy. Is there a request of yourself that comes from the energy itself?

Take some time to write down in your journal any request that may have emerged for you or share your request with your partner.

No matter what is going on in the body or in the awareness, it exists in and through us as an encompassing, invisible, silent presence. Presence is in our inner space and in the space all around us. As we sense into presence, there is a quality of aliveness; it's awake, aware. This presence has no name. Our lives exist in this natural grace of presence that doesn't change no matter what we do.

---

What serves us is a deep, intuitive trusting in life, and a plunging into our own bodily felt experience with the clear intention for heart-centered presence with ourselves and with another.

## CHAPTER FOUR

# Life Unfiltered

When the truth of love comes, when the real intimacy arises between human beings and the universe itself, that intimacy and that truth are felt. They aren't known conceptually. They arise through the body. So, when we speak of turning to God, when we speak of turning to the infinite one, when we talk of ending separation, they may be ideas and hopefully those ideas serve as inspiration to go on. But the real prayer, the real movement is one in which we turn the attention to the body. Because it is in the body and only in the body that the bliss of union is going to be felt. And not in the mind.

In some very real sense, the mind is totally transformed by a return of the attention to the heart. It becomes a different instrument altogether. It isn't gone, but the function that we have assigned to the mind in our separated state is no longer a useful function at all. The oppressive veil of thought dissolves and in its place, we find that the eyes open into the spaciousness of the heart. The ears open into the spaciousness of the heart. The tongue, the sense of touch, all life . . . instead of being filtered through a sensory mechanism caught in thought, redesigned, and then experienced is suddenly experienced directly through the heart. And it does not encounter density but rather encounters a lucid open space, in which nothing is caught in definition. Nothing is caught in the past, nothing is caught in

> the confines of imposed reality but is rather allowed to move and change and reorganize itself in the great space of the living presence that dwells in the body, in the heart, and in the heart of all hearts. This is what we long for as feeling beings in the realm of mystery.
>
> —STEPHEN SCHWARTZ[5]

CULTIVATING OUR OBSERVING awareness and increasing our understanding of the thinking mind are two elements I find to be essential in the work of Living Compassion and Nonviolent Communication. This quote from Stephen Schwartz expresses something important and eloquent in relation to the work we are doing and to its essential, spiritual aspect.

What stands out for me in this reading, and what I'd like to emphasize, has to do with the functioning of the thinking mind when it's in a separated state. Thought can be one of the obstacles to fully connecting. The kind of thoughts and thinking patterns that become obstacles are those that arise when we are in judgment, when we are evaluating, and when we are in analytical and intellectual thought, separate from the body.

In contrast, the kind of thoughts Stephen talks about in this quote are those that arise when we are centered in our consciousness and fully experiencing life from the perspective of dwelling in the heart. Thought doesn't go away; it is transformed. Its function changes and it becomes an instrument of the heart.

## WHERE WE PUT OUR ATTENTION

In our work of self-compassion there is a subtle distinction between observing awareness and the thinking mind. Awareness is something we observe *with*; it is the context or the medium that forms the basis of all our experiencing. The content is the form of our experience.

It's not the mind that observes; it's awareness that observes. One of our primary challenges occurs when we mix up our thoughts with awareness. When we observe something and intertwine it with our thoughts about what we observe, this mixture becomes an obstacle to fully experiencing *what is*.

Thoughts and all other forms of experiencing—such as emotional feeling, bodily sensations, and the life force moving in and through our Being and manifesting as our needs and values—are the *objects* of that awareness. The subtle, formless container of all experiencing is awareness itself. Awareness is what sheds light on the thoughts. We call this "the light of awareness."

Awareness is attention. The quality of our experience, and therefore the quality of our lives, is a function of how we focus our attention.

Many years ago, at a pivotal point in my development, I discovered that all practice is the discipline of attention; it is not just the form that supports attention. For example, I can do a yoga practice or any number of other practices, but fundamentally at the heart of any practice is the discipline of attention—how I focus my awareness—and the link and connection my attention has to energy or experience. The fundamental core of my practice is seated in my awareness and how I direct my awareness to my experiencing.

The practices I present here are fundamentally a cultivating of my attention and my awareness. The meditation and mindfulness teacher Sarah McLean talks about attention in a similar way:

> Your attention is powerful, full of power. The kind of attention I am talking about is your non-judgmental, welcoming, loving attention. This attention energizes and enlivens all things in your life. Your attention arises from inside you, from that presence we'll call your "inner self." What you pay attention to and how you pay attention is how you use your power. When you reclaim your attention, you reclaim your power, your true power, and this leads to a peaceful and more fulfilling and creative life.[6]

Sarah's words communicate an essential aspect of the cultivation, development, and practice of cultivating presence through the transformational spiritual practices such as self-compassion.

## CULTIVATING OBSERVING AWARENESS THROUGH SELF-COMPASSION

In the course of living, there is a continual dance between the exterior of life and how we receive and experience it with our interior impressions. These impressions contain energetic, living information. How we attend to these impressions is the fundamental focus of this work of Living Compassion. Another way to express this is with the adage "It's not what happens to you; it's what you do with what happens to you." It may be relatively easy to intellectually understand that our perspective affects our experience, but it can be a challenge to know it experientially. When we mix in our evaluations, our judgments, and our reactions about what happens to us with what we observe, this creates disconnection, distress, and suffering.

What I've learned is that whatever arises in us is, to some degree, either heaven or hell. It's hell to the degree that we buy into it, struggle with it, repress it, don't want to accept it but want it to be something different. That's hellish! But it's heaven to the extent that we can take everything that arises—judgments and everything—as invitations to listen deeply to those parts of ourselves that don't know how to express themselves other than as judgments right now.

The nature of self-compassion and self-connection is the foundation of our living and of how we communicate. The basic dynamic of self-compassion is cultivating our ability to inhabit observing awareness. We then establish an intimate relationship between the one who observes and the interior experience or content we are observing.

When we become conscious that we are dwelling in the observing awareness, it's not so much that we're observing our awareness but that the awareness itself is who we are. I've heard the expression "I become aware of awareness" countless times before, but we're not *observing* our awareness in that sense. We *are* awareness. We are dwelling in the observing awareness, and we are resting in it. This is a little different from the observing awareness that observes the content of our experience. It doesn't matter whether the content is flowing and radiant or obstructive and constricted. We're observing while experiencing at the same time. It is not one or the other that is happening.

When we are dwelling in the observing awareness, there is always a form of experiencing. It is not an either-or situation. We are dwelling in the sense of presence, and presence is always recognizing our experience and is aware of life as it unfolds. The more we are in presence, the more there is flow, equanimity, peace. We are observing while experiencing the content at the same time. It is not just one or the other that is happening. These two dimensions are so inextricably intertwined that it's a challenge to discern the distinction between them. The interfusion between them is so subtle; it requires a considerable amount of practice and skill to develop the clarity of what can be called a "differentiated unity." When we have this unity of awareness and experiencing, our mind becomes creative and inspired because it is seated in the essential consciousness of the heart itself.

When I am in an unobstructed state of Being—experiencing thoughts and judgments and observing them at the same time—there is a wholeness and a differentiation within that unity.

## PRESENCE AND EXPERIENCING

There are two primary dimensions in observing and experiencing: the observing awareness and the form or content of experiencing. These two dimensions are inextricably interwoven. I've created a conceptual framework for understanding these two dimensions that I call "Presence and Experiencing." Although these lists are presented side by side, there is no correspondence between the "Presence" list on the left and the "Experiencing" list on the right. The relationship is that "formless" is the observer and "form" is that which is observed.

| PRESENCE | EXPERIENCING |
|---|---|
| **Formless** | **Form** |
| Awareness | Thinking, Imagining, and Emotion |
| Witnessing | Sensation and Sensing (*dense and subtle*) |
| Noticing | Longing and Yearning |
| Attention | Valuing and Needing |
| Attending To | Acting and Behaving (*includes speaking*) |
| Being With | |

Presence is formless. Awareness (as well as all the other words listed under "Presence," which for our purposes are synonymous) is an expression of the nature of presence. Presence is always witnessing, noticing, attending to, and being with. The more in presence we are, the more there is flow, equanimity, and peace. One of the reasons I use a variety of words for the same experience is that different words connote different meanings for people. Consider the words *witnessing*, *observing*, and *noticing*. For me, the experience is the same for all of these, only the words are different.

Experiencing, on the other hand, has content and form. These include the cognitive dimension of thinking and imagining, the emotional dimension, and the sensation dimension that includes experiencing along a spectrum of dense and subtle sensing. This is the experience of the life force as it moves through the body; through thinking, feeling, and sensing, and it manifests as a longing or yearning of the heart, in the form of what we value and need. Experiencing includes the observable behaviors of whatever we do when we take action, including speaking and listening.

If I have an experience in which I am triggered and pain is stimulated, I first want to acknowledge that I am experiencing a state of contraction.

That acknowledgment is an important form of observing awareness. With it, I've begun the self-compassion process. Everything I do internally, anything I focus my awareness on, is in relationship to the reactive state I've just acknowledged. I breathe. My intention is to allow whatever is arising in me to be just as it is. When judgments are there, I recognize them. When the reactive contraction of my feelings—such as fear, anger, or overwhelm—is there, I recognize this. When sensations are there, I recognize them. It may take a bit of time just to focus my attention on this inner process. Bringing my awareness to my thoughts, feelings, and sensations happens before I connect to my longings. At the very heart of this reactive state is the beauty of my unmet needs, the life force itself. This is the second stream of Living Compassion.

By focusing my awareness on my internal experiencing and the reactive state, I am cultivating and developing this observing awareness. Now, my reactive state may not transform immediately, but when I reside in the observing awareness, that in and of itself begins to yield the transformational process. It unfolds; it is a yielding experience. For example, when I stay with and compassionately embrace my initial reactive feeling of anger, it will always unfold into fear. It may start as a frozen fear, but if I can stay with it, a softening occurs, and gradually it will resolve into what I describe as a soft, vulnerable fear. In the experience of fear, there may be other painful emotions that I want to notice and allow, embrace and feel. At the heart of these emotions is always a link to my deep needs. When I can connect to the energy of my needs, for me, this is the beginning of the restoration of my wholeness.

## TWO-MINUTE SELF-COMPASSION

My capacity to be empathic with someone is founded on my ability to connect with myself. When I receive a reaction from another person, I first want to take time to sit with myself and identify specifically what this person said. I want to bring my attention to my inner reaction, to open to it and allow it, to let myself feel the pain or anything else I may be feeling. I want to transform my judgments, to be aware of bodily sensations, and to connect to the longings and needs that are not being fulfilled in this interaction.

Staying with the pain of our reactions can be hard. If you find it difficult, it would be valuable to pay attention to that and to ask yourself, "What are the first moments in my experience of inner compassion that are difficult, and what am I telling myself? That I'm not able to do it?" Identify and remember those first moments. They can give you a clue about what you can do. Maybe you will realize that you are not capable of being empathic at this time. Can you stand back and see what thoughts you are telling yourself?

This is an initial step of self-compassion, and it takes place in your own space. You are not in the relational space because you are not able to access your resources for empathy. A principle I learned many years ago in NVC is that I can't offer empathy if I'm in pain or triggered. I don't have the resources. I have to restore myself through self-empathy or through receiving it from someone else before I can offer empathy to another.

In the midst of everyday life, even in the midst of focused activity, there is a form of self-care you can explore that can transform your experience. Pause for two minutes . . . that is all, just pause for two minutes. Take those minutes to stop and notice what you are feeling. Pause. Notice your body, and name what you sense. Notice what you are feeling emotionally. Notice what you are telling yourself.

That's all. It's a simple practice. I'm not saying it is easy. I think it takes commitment to give yourself two or three minutes to pause . . . to simply notice . . . and ask yourself, "What am I feeling and needing?"

Our life is a meditation. The question is, moment by moment, day by day, where is our attention? What are we meditating? Are we aware of the flow of life? As an inquiry, can we bring awareness and mindfulness into every moment of living? We can choose to have a conscious, deliberate intention to focus our attention on presence and authenticity. But if we are not meditating on something focused, directed, conscious, present . . . guess what we are meditating on? We are meditating on the relatively unconscious habituation of a mind in separation. The deliberate intention to stay consciously participating in the flow of life involves noticing the moment when we get disconnected and then reconnecting to the flow of life.

## A SEPARATED STATE OF MIND

It is important to understand the nature of the thinking mind when it is in what I call a separated state and to recognize when that separation has occurred. When we can recognize that our thinking mind is in separation, then we are able to make a more conscious choice with regard to it.

The mind filters and mediates experience so we do not experience life directly but indirectly. When we are in a separated state, our mind distorts and filters experience. In the separated state, our mind is influenced by the life experiences that we carry within our system that were conscious or unconscious mental creations. We know the thinking mind is in a separated state when it fears the unknown; it is uncomfortable with what is unfamiliar.

Two different aspects influence the tendency of the mind to mediate and distort. The first is that all the traumatic and painful experiences we've had become internalized beliefs that then have a mediating function. The second is that the mind creates identity, or we can say the mind creates self-identity. When we identify with a conditioned pattern of experiences that we take ourselves to be, we become fundamentally identified with a constellation of self-images and self-concepts. We take ourselves to be this. We become identified with this, and it can be very limiting. Again, there is no judgment in identifying ourselves in this way. It doesn't mean there's something wrong or bad when we are engaged in our personal identity.

The interpretive mind believes that our mediated experiences are reality. One of the fundamental differentiations in Nonviolent Communication is that when we mix our evaluations with our observations, we believe in our thoughts. Someone says or does something in relation to me or someone else that stimulates pain, and my mind says, "This person is mean and inconsiderate." I become identified with that thought and, in other words, I believe that it is true. This is one of the ways our thinking mind functions. We take our interpretations to be the truth rather than looking at what is observed and calling that the truth. This is how the separated, interpretive mind takes mediated experiences to be reality.

Can you notice how this may be occurring in your own experience?

Our tendency to judge can be very powerful. Even though we might find ourselves in judging, reactive states, it can be very challenging to transform them because there is a certain inertia to reactivity that, in my experience, is based on survival.

## THE SURVIVAL TENDENCY OF THE SEPARATED MIND

The primary purpose of the mind is to survive, to perpetuate its own existence. We are familiar with our mind; it can be seen as our comfort zone. When we are in the defensive, judgmental mode of a separated state, there is a part of our mind that wants to justify, defend, attack, rebel, attempt to be right, and maintain the status quo. This part of our mind we identify with is attached to the familiar and the known, and it's this part that is uncomfortable with what is unknown.

Stephen Schwartz also addresses the survival aspect of the mind:

> The ego mechanism [which I, Robert, see as the protective and defensive survival structures] seems to be helpful because it pushes down what otherwise would seem to be unutterably painful. Our life here is tragic in this respect. We feel we are separated forever . . . from mother, father, universe, and must make it without help. And the ego keeps us always in exile. Our true being longs for freedom.[7]

In many spiritual approaches and traditions, this survival tendency of the mind is traditionally called the "ego." My understanding of the ego, however, is different from this. For me, the ego is not some nasty enemy I have to transcend and get over because it is keeping me unenlightened and imprisoned in dark places. I see the ego as the part of our system that has developed based on conditioning from our culture and on the many painful experiences we've had in our lives. The ego serves to protect us from pain and whatever seems threatening, so we will defend ourselves against perceived danger. This protection often looks like an ego-based reaction or defense.

But then there is the kind of thought that arises in my mind when I am connected to my heart, whether I am feeling some intense experience or not, and this kind of thought rings true. A clarity arises, and there is a deep "yes" that I feel in my Being. This is what I call "inspired thought." The thought in and of itself isn't necessarily a unified, embodied experience, but it can lead and inspire me into cultivating this experience and living in this way.

For example, if I have an inspired thought, a recognition that I'm innocent, that we all are innocent, this doesn't necessarily mean I'm going to experience someone's innocence when they say something that stimulates pain in me. But this recognition of innocence serves as an inner guidepost. I can say to myself, "Ah, I remember I am innocent. I remember the other person is innocent. What does that mean?" This inner dialogue inspires me to listen and find the other person's innocence in what they are saying and look for my own innocence in my reaction. Inspired thought becomes a guide, making this kind of thought and inner dialogue very useful.

## BRINGING SELF-COMPASSION TO OUR REACTIVITY

I want to unpack the fundamental practice of self-compassion using this diagram I refer to as "The Life Process in Reaction." It is impossible to create a structure that replicates an internal, subjective experience, but this is my attempt to do that.

At the top of the diagram is an image of a cloud that represents an event or a stimulus occurring at any given time in our life. This life

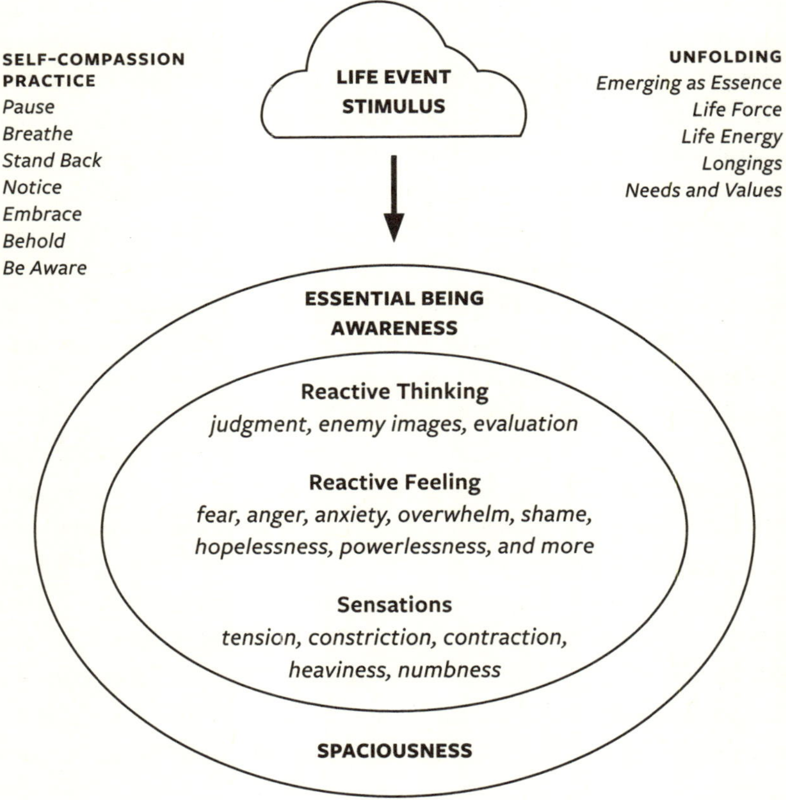


event is something we receive, and it enters into the circle below it, which represents the container of our life experiences. As the arrow indicates, the stimulus enters into us through our awareness and our essential Being. The amount of spaciousness we have regarding the stimulus will depend on our level of awareness and to what extent we are identified with reactive experiencing.

The center of the diagram describes the content of our experience when we are in a reactive, separated state, which takes the form of our reactive thoughts, such as judgments and evaluations; our reactive feelings such as fear, anxiety, or overwhelm; and our reactive sensations, such as tension, contraction, constriction, heaviness, or sometimes numbness. There is an intimate relationship we develop with ourselves between our awareness, which is our essential Being, and the content of our reactions.

What we are cultivating in Living Compassion is "the one who compassionately observes." The more I am able to dwell in awareness, notice compassionately, and embrace my internal reaction with a spaciousness that allows transformation to take place, the more I develop the center of gravity within myself of the one who compassionately observes. The more I practice this, the more I have available the capacity to be present and compassionate with my own inner experience and with others.

The words on the right side of the cloud describe awareness and what emerges from it. The more I cultivate awareness, I become in touch with a life force or energy that takes the form of my heart's longings, what I am needing and valuing, and what matters to me as a form of life reaching for life. This connection to the life force becomes more available to me as I develop a compassionate, witnessing experience.

The words on the left side of the cloud describe some of the primary elements of this self-compassion practice, which is simply a practice of inner noticing and embracing. When we think of embracing, many of us may think of hugging someone or something. What I mean in this diagram is a subtler kind of embracing.

If I "behold" something in front of me, I notice it is there. It is alive and it is real. I take it all in—I behold it, I witness it, I observe it, I notice it is there, alive, and real. When I am beholding fully, there is no part of my attention that is elsewhere. For example, if I am in a museum and I see a work of art that my mind would evaluate as incredible and inspiring, I would stand in front of this artwork and breathe. I would experience awe as I beheld this piece of art. This experience of beholding is a kind of cherishing, where I allow all of my attention to be there, present to the art.

As I behold something, I am embracing it with my full awareness, with my full heart. There's an intimacy between me and the object that

I am beholding. I am close to it. I embrace it with gentleness, kindness, inclusion. For me, there is no distinction between beholding and embracing; these are simply metaphors, because experience itself goes beyond the physicality where metaphors reside.

In our practice of self-compassion, we always want to remember to pause first and breathe. Breathing changes the physiology of reactivity into a more receptive state. Then, metaphorically, we want to stand back, because a little distance is required as we begin observing. We can then remember to notice, behold, and embrace whatever experiencing we have in our awareness. We want to be aware.

## A DISCERNING AWARENESS

Presence is not something we do; it is something we allow. Revisiting the "Presence and Experiencing" diagram, we can see that the quality of presence is formless. When we observe presence, we see that it is infinite. It goes beyond us. Our thinking, conditioned mind will argue with anything, but presence does not argue. Presence simply allows.

Cultivating inner presence involves an intention and commitment to being watchfully aware, moment by moment. It's important to recognize when we are in the flow of life and when we are not in the flow of life. When we do this, we can recognize experientially that we are sometimes in an unrestricted feeling flow or a contracted state, or maybe we are experiencing a combination of both.

"Am I enjoying myself?" is a helpful inquiry. "What needs are alive or not alive in me right now? What do I choose at this moment?" These inquiries bring a living awareness that reveals to me my needs that are met and unmet and to what extent I am in a life flow. I can then consciously choose to be with the life in me, to mourn or to celebrate, and to take action or not.

This awareness is watchfulness. It is a nonjudging but discerning awareness. We want to remain present and alive to the flow of consciousness and living energy as it flows through us, moment by moment. Even in this moment, as you read this, see if you can feel the energy as it moves through your awareness. What are the qualities of this energy? Perhaps the energy of care? Of clarity? Of inspiration? By cultivating inner presence, we recognize and remain in the flow of life.

The two dimensions of observing awareness and the content of our experiencing are so inextricably intertwined that it's a challenge to discern the distinction between them. The interfusion between them is so subtle; I cannot experience something without being aware of it.

When I am engaged in witnessing my observing awareness in relation to what I am experiencing, the quality of my experience is enhanced, enriched, and made fuller. There is more flow as I do this. It affects the quality of my experiencing.

## DEVELOPING CAPACITY

I can be in a separated reactive state, or I can be in an undefended state with my heart open. People sometimes ask if it is possible to reside permanently in a vulnerable, undefended state. I don't reside in that state permanently, but I think it is possible. But living in an undefended and therefore authentic state permanently isn't the main point of what we are doing with these spiritual practices.

Our work here has to do with the concept of development. I'll use an analogy of physical exercise to illustrate this. If I want to be fit, and I am fifty pounds heavier than my ideal weight, I can work on my diet and exercise, and I can become more fit. Now, developing the physical body is different from the movements in our psychological states, but there is a degree of similarity with improving well-being through exercise and diet. To sustain what could be called the "cherished" or "valued" state requires that I maintain my diet and exercise practice. If I let go of that practice, then I'm going to slide back into the previous state.

Consciousness can be seen as a psychological state instead of the physical one we used in the example. There is a developmental process in which the more I practice, the more my center of gravity begins to shift into the transformed state of being in the flow of life, residing in my heart in nonreactive, undefended wholeness.

Maintaining and sustaining a practice is required to shift the center of my gravity from one that is predominantly identified in the reactive state with core beliefs and traumatic patterns to one in which I am more and more present within myself.

I've discovered that with a dedicated and committed practice, we can shift into a state of living preponderantly in our wholeness. When this happens, it doesn't mean we don't shift back into other states, but the more we practice, the more we find ourselves dwelling in fullness and wholeness.

I remember being asked, "Do you get triggered anymore?" That's easy to answer: "Of course I do!" But over time I've noticed that there are three characteristics of how this shift toward fullness and wholeness manifests. First, the frequency of being triggered is reduced. Second, the intensity of my reaction is much less, and I don't get lost in it as much as I did in the past. And third, the duration of my triggered state is significantly less.

I think it is beneficial to see this shift toward wholeness as a development, as something we practice, not as a goal of residing in some permanent state. As I've mentioned earlier, seeking any specific outcome has the drawback of coming from deficiency, the orientation exemplified by "I'm not there yet" thinking. Instead of always trying to reach and seek from a sense of something missing—grasping outside myself in my relationships or in my life—we can relax that grasping and come to the realization that what we seek is the pathway to our own heart.

## MEDITATION

### *Awareness*

**You might want to record the following meditation first and then play it to guide you. Spend time with and notice whatever is present after each question or reflection.**

**There is a principle in this meditation: Whatever arises, you allow it to be there, embrace it, and love it just as it is. Open to it, bring compassion to it.**

---

Let's begin.

I invite you to close your eyes, settle, and get comfortable in your seat, sitting as straight as you can.

Bring attention to your body and to your breath. Simply acknowledge your awareness. Breathe and rest in your awareness. Notice that your awareness surrounds and imbues all that you are experiencing: your breath . . . your body . . . the environment. Can you sense the container of your awareness?

Whatever arises in your experience, simply be aware of it. Thoughts, images, emotional feelings, bodily sensations, and longings are always in movement—they flow and change.

Awareness is unmoving. It is always here as a presence, encompassing, embracing, outside of time and space. Refrain from trying to understand this with your mind.

I invite you to notice as much as you can. There is such an intimate, intertwined, co-arising of awareness itself in all the forms of your experiencing. Awareness is always present, even when you don't notice it.

As you rest in your awareness, embracing and allowing the flow of all your experience without resisting it, find your strength, your power, and your equanimity. Feel your aliveness . . .

Whenever you are ready, slowly move your attention back into the space where you are. Allow yourself to take a deeper breath, and then open your eyes. You may want to write about your experience of awareness before continuing to explore noticing in your journal.

JOURNAL

## *Noticing*

**This practice cultivates our ability to just notice, which is an element of our awareness. It is an invitation to be aware of the act of experiencing itself, whatever thoughts, images, feelings, sensations, or longings are there.**

**Take a moment to step back and notice whatever you can of your internal experiencing. Now notice that you are being aware of that.**

**If you are doing this practice alone, it can be helpful to use a journal to note down your responses to the prompts. If you are practicing with a partner, you can share your responses aloud.**

---

Let's begin.

I invite you to bring your attention to your body and to your breath. Relax and breathe.

Now focus your attention on your present-moment experience, whatever it is. If it's a stimulated, triggered state, then so be it. Notice whatever you are experiencing.

As you pay attention to what you are experiencing right now, notice and identify any thoughts, images, or stories. Journal or share this aloud if you are doing this practice with a partner.

Notice and identify any emotional feelings. What are you feeling now? Notice if what you are feeling changes as you pay attention to it. Then journal or share aloud with your partner.

Notice and identify sensations. Take your time; there's no rush. Feel whatever you are sensing and journal or share this with your partner.

Notice, acknowledge, and identify whatever is alive in you in terms of your needs, your longings, what you value, and what matters to you at this moment in your life. Journal or share this aloud.

Now notice your awareness that contains all of your experiencing. "Step back" and sense the content of your awareness, even as it moves and changes its shape. Notice the content of all your experience . . .

all your thoughts, the whole constellation of feelings, sensations, and the energy of your needs. This is the subtlest step. You are noticing all your experience and then recognizing and witnessing that it is your awareness that contains this experiencing.

Now bring your attention back to the content of your experiencing. You are simply moving your attention back and forth between the awareness that is doing the noticing and the forms of experiencing being noticed. If you can, notice the interfusion of the observing awareness and the form of experiencing (thoughts, feelings, sensations, and longings). This is a subtle process . . . moving back and forth or even simultaneously.

Complete this practice by journaling or sharing with your partner whatever is arising in you.

---

I would characterize my life practice as a continual, embodied mindfulness. I'm not bopping along in my life . . . doing okay . . . then I get triggered, and I say to myself, "Okay, now it's time to practice self-compassion." That is not how I experience a spiritual life practice.

Living Compassion is my continual, embodied mindfulness practice because the longing in my Being is to live and feel the fullness and the freedom every moment of my life. The continual sense of intimacy with the life in me is a way of living. As the clinical psychologist Laurence Heller has said, "The price of freedom is eternal mindfulness."[8] I want to live mindful, aware, and free at every moment.

CHAPTER FIVE

# From Resisting to Embracing Life

Can we see directly into what our experience is without trying to modify it, improve it, change it, condition it, without searching for the pleasure, pushing away the pain? We constantly generate descriptions by which we live. We know that life is not contained within the conceptual realm; it is not described accurately by those ideas, yet we live in relationship to those ideas.

At every moment we have the capacity to fall back into the defended space of the known and we have the ability to abandon the moment and enter into the unknown of what is next. Let us face the full range of the human potential by engaging the fear of a negative expression and the attraction of a positive expression, both of which are terrifying. We are as afraid of our love as we are of our anger. The expression of the unknown is a deep feeling . . . not feeling in terms of emotion, which is also conditioned just like thought is, but feeling that is the totality of the energetic movement in the system expressing itself through some aspect. This is a radical life. While it is fresh and alive, it may be totally unrecognizable to us to be completely authentic in the moment.

—STEVEN HARRISON[9]

FUNDAMENTAL TO THIS process we call Nonviolent Communication and this body of work I call Living Compassion is our relationship to what arises within us as we receive life—how we meet life's energies as we experience them in all their forms, whether from other people or our own choices about what we do and say. We are cultivating our capacity to embrace these energies with compassion as they occur in the ever-changing landscape of our inner lives.

## IMPERMANENCE

The nature of life is ever-changing. We understand this conceptually when we observe life and see things around us constantly change. In fact, everything changes. Some things change at a faster pace than others. Things change in the exterior world, and our interior experiencing is also always changing and moving.

Related to this worldview is a Buddhist concept known as impermanence. Living with impermanence means living with the understanding and acceptance that everything changes; everything comes and goes. It means living in the awareness that everything flows, everything is constantly moving and changing in our inner and outer lives.

To stay in the present moment, living in and from our center, requires accepting and not resisting change as it occurs. That is easy to say and perhaps conceptually easy to understand, but it is another thing altogether to experience. I like what philosopher Alan Watts says about the inevitability of change and the discomfort that arises with it: "The only way to make sense out of change is to plunge into it, move with it, and join the dance."[10] I invite you to notice within yourself the nature of change and how you meet it.

## OPEN TO LIFE

What is the significance of accepting that which I experience, whether it's something I enjoy or something I find uncomfortable? The more I grow in my capacity to live with impermanence, the more I am able to embrace my unmet needs. This means being comfortable with discomfort, with what is unwanted. The poet Henry Wadsworth Longfellow put this simply: "For after all, the best thing one can do when it is raining is to let it rain."[11] Resistance is like railing against the rain, trying to move the stream of life in the opposite direction. I want to notice any resistance and become curious about the part of me that is resisting. I notice that in my mind, the part of me that resists is holding on to what is familiar and known.

Relationships change. We grow apart, we lose connections. We come together, we reestablish trust, and we strengthen our connections. Accepting change is accepting outer circumstances and accepting the inner experience of what is unexpected or unwanted.

One of the ways I know I am resisting instead of accepting change is that there's a part of me that wants to manage and control what is occurring or what is arising within me. I want to fix it and to make it better. This response comes from the energy of resistance.

When I experience something unpleasant or uncomfortable, what follows is either the unobstructed natural pain as the situation arises or a resistance to my experience of pain that leads to suffering. When I am in the suffering state, I am resisting the natural flow of life. To be open to a life experience is to feel it in an undefended way, and that requires my vulnerability. This is what I mean when I say, "I'm not resisting."

As the author John Green said, "When you stopped wishing things wouldn't fall apart, you'd stop suffering when they did."[12] This seems to be part of the human condition. When things fall apart and don't go the way we want them to go, this brings up our suffering, mostly because we have not yet developed the capacity to be with and embrace the experience we call pain.

## ACCEPTANCE IS NOT RESIGNATION

This work of creating a space of compassion is founded on accepting and welcoming what is, both in the exterior world and as things arise within us. When I talk about accepting, I'm not talking about agreeing with anything or anyone. If something happens or someone says something I am uncomfortable with, accepting it doesn't signify that I agree with or condone what was said or done. I am not saying, "It's okay." If I condone something, this could lead to an experience of resignation, which is a misinterpretation of what I mean by acceptance.

So when I accept something, this doesn't mean I am resigned to it. Resignation feels and sounds like giving up: "Oh, what's the use? I might as well accept it. There's nothing I can do about it anyway. The situation is hopeless . . ." When I am resigned or I condone something, I feel a particular quality of energy in my body—a sinking down, a sense of giving up—that restricts the flow of life as it moves through me. This energy affects my experience of openness. Instead of resonance, I feel a dissonance within.

When I am accepting or allowing something, I want to ask myself, "What is it I am letting go of?" One of the things I let go of when I am in acceptance is the tendency to try to manage and control. I am not resigned to the situation—I am accepting that I cannot control it, and I allow the flow of life to move through me.

Accepting is an invitation to feel what is present without resisting it. I allow myself to feel the energy and intensity of my experience. When I do this, I am cultivating more room inside of myself and in my capacity to feel energy, to feel life. I am welcoming life.

## WELCOMING ALL OF LIFE

I've discovered that if I want to welcome life and to be in an inner state of freedom with respect to all the experiences of life, then I must learn how to embrace discomfort. I want to learn how to allow and to feel the intensity of sensation that is at the heart of anything uncomfortable. To do this, I just stay with my inner experiencing. I don't push myself *into* the experience of pain but gently stay *with* it.

When I am able to stay with the intensity at the core of discomfort, what is likely to happen in my system is that a profound inner part of me says, "No! Don't go there!" This part comes from my history and conditioning, and it learned how to protect and defend me from feeling anything that was uncomfortable. Cultivating our capacity to tolerate discomfort relaxes our fears and grows our inner freedom to embrace more of life.

Whenever there's an intensity, what it shows me is that something really matters to me; there is something that I care about. Intensity shows me what the value is in what matters to me. I have the choice to look beneath the discomfort or to let my mind take over and resist it while judging myself (or other people) or feeling overwhelmed. There's a choice point here. The experience of intensity is life speaking to me. It is the energy of my needs speaking to me. Can I connect to life? As much as I can, I want to stay in tune with the energy of this intensity that is taking me to what I am needing and valuing.

If I stay in the intensity of an experience to the limit of my capacity to tolerate it, I remember I can back off. I can breathe. I can remember that there is no urgency, even though the intensity of the pain might be pushing me toward immediate release. I want to remember and recognize these compassion practices: *I can be patient, I don't need to push myself*, and *I can breathe.*

At every moment, I want to be as present, relaxed, and open as I am able to be—the first stream of Living Compassion. Whenever I am not able to be in this state, I want to be with that inability—the second stream of Living Compassion. I let myself feel the discomfort and resistance to my limited capacity, with as much openness and care as I bring to all the elements of my experience.

## TURNING TOWARD PAIN

Emotional pain, in NVC terms, arises when something happens that surrounds something we care about in which our needs aren't met. Given our conditioning, embracing pain is seemingly counterintuitive. Our mind might even see the concept of embracing pain as masochistic: "What do you mean *enjoy* pain?" So, turning toward pain is a radical approach to our conditioning and to the survival mechanisms embedded in us from the culture and our training that tell us to make pain go away and to hang on to pleasure.

The brain is wired for biological and physical survival. And I want to acknowledge that there's a distinction between physical survival and psychological survival. Somehow, when we perceive an emotional or psychological threat, the biological survival process that exists in the brain as a natural and necessary part of human functioning gets confused and transposes emotional survival into physical survival. This activates reactions that would be helpful in physical survival, but it limits the quality of our experience when there is a perceived emotional threat.

The mind's confusion between physical and psychological survival gives rise to psychological defense mechanisms that keep us emotionally closed and unable to be vulnerable. This can happen because we perceive—based on conditioning and past trauma—that something is a threat to our physical existence. On some level, our Being, our consciousness, believes there is a threat to our survival, and we react with the kind of strength and force needed to protect our life.

There is still a lot of depth to the exploration of trauma and how it activates the separated state and that survival part of the brain, usurping the power of the cognitive mind so that we act as if we need to physically survive.

From the aspects of physical survival and physical well-being, within the natural order of things, there is something life-serving about resistance to pain. We don't want to perpetuate the pain if we can support ourselves in our well-being. But this tendency starts to reinforce itself in very deep, unconscious, and habitual ways when physical pain translates into emotional and psychological pain. We then develop a view of ourselves and of life that tells us that we are not able to tolerate the intensity of discomfort. At the heart of much of my emotional pain, my psychological pain, is the need to feel safe and secure, which usually means some kind of comfort with the familiar and the known.

When we unfold the core of our Being, we find that our true self carries qualities such as compassion and freedom. But these qualities are often covered up by the layers of pain and contraction that we've accumulated. This is not just emotional; it's felt in the body as a physical sensation of holding back, of being bound by something unseen yet deeply present.

Physical pain is often related to the needs of the body for physical health and sustenance, while emotional pain can often be seen as our interpretation or story about what is happening. When we go into that emotional experience with openness, we allow the life force to "wash through" us, and we can experience it as energy rather than a painful story or resistance. For me to experience an energetic washing through, I have to be open and vulnerable to the entirety of the feeling, allowing both physical and emotional pain to be present and flow together. Resistance to one can block the other, and feeling fully requires a holistic acceptance of both.

When I have emotional resistance to physical pain, it creates suffering beyond just the physical experience. Emotional resistance might sound like, "Oh my God! What is this?! Why won't it go away? Now I'm miserable! I can't do what I wanted to do!" These kinds of thoughts can go on and on and on. When I take a moment to stay with the experience of physical pain before I act automatically, I find that I can create a space in which I do not emotionally resist the physical pain. This space affects my experience of physical pain.

## DISCOVERING THE PRECIOUS LIFE WITHIN PAIN

Experiencing life, I am engaging in life: hearing it, receiving it, and participating in it. When I tune in to life energy on a felt, energetic level, I am paying attention to it. By paying attention to the life force, I am more likely to be able to stay in the flow of this energy rather than resist it. I don't have any control over the existence of the life force. It is just here. What I do have a choice over is how I meet the life force.

The energy of life manifests through us and throughout everything. So the choice is either to go on with my conditioning to obstruct it, which is usually unconscious and habituated, or to develop my capacity to live in the flow. I can do this by slowly, gently, and compassionately recognizing obstructions and simply allowing them. Life shows me over and over again that at the heart of those obstructions is precious life reaching for life.

I want to remember the principle that whenever I am experiencing pain, it is because of my precious unmet need. I want to know this cognitively and in an embodied way. As I develop this capacity for self-compassion, I begin to notice when I feel something uncomfortable (a restriction, something that I don't enjoy), and I start to move toward it with trust. I become curious. I am aware I have a choice.

Gradually and with practice, as I move toward pain, I realize that it is not the inner enemy. The pain is not a "bad" part of me trying to make my life miserable. It is simply an aspect of me. Increasingly, as I learn how to approach my inner pain, I begin to be compassionate with those parts of myself that I previously ran away from when I didn't have the capacity to be with and feel my pain. I begin to befriend myself. This is a form of self-love. I am developing an intimate relationship with myself.

I find using inquiries helpful for inviting clarity and connection with myself. A couple of inquiries that have helped me with self-compassion are: *How can I be in an intimate nonviolent, compassionate relationship with someone else unless I am able to be compassionate and nonviolent with all parts of myself? How can I be with somebody without pushing them away if I can't be with myself without pushing parts of myself away?*

Love is attention. Love is awareness: nonjudgmental, accepting, allowing awareness. Love is a component of compassion. Like love, compassion is infinitely patient. It doesn't push me into anything. It allows.

## MOVING TOWARD SELF-CARE

I want to be aware if I am avoiding something out of fear or if I am moving toward something from a space of self-connection. There's no right or wrong way. I want to be conscious of the motivation that is moving me toward whatever choice or strategy I am making.

For me, if I am moving toward something, the motivating energy is always care. If I am moving away from something, the motivating energy is always fear. If the energy is fear, I want to notice it. The fear is inviting me. It is calling me. It is needing and wanting compassion. This process is an invitation to feel life.

If I am fearful, I want to allow myself to feel fearful, to let myself connect with it. I ask myself, "What is the part of me that is afraid?" For example, it may be that I am not fully trusting that I will be able to maintain my center and my presence when I hear this other person speak to me. I'm not confident they are going to communicate with me in a way that is fully considerate and respectful of me and in which I will be seen.

I want to transform my fear as much as I can with self-empathy, because this will help me to move toward what I care about, what I am valuing and needing. Remember, fear is often connected with a need for safety. I want to examine what I am telling myself about this fear. What are my thoughts and beliefs about safety and security? This is an important inquiry to explore. The more we do this, the more we find this source of safety and security is already within us. Don't let go of that. Instead, let go of the externally referenced need that we can only feel safe if something in our environment is a certain way.

It feels so good to move toward something, toward self-care. When I'm taking care of myself, I feel empowered. I have found this practice is especially important in situations where my choices seem limited.

## CELEBRATING THE ALIVENESS IN SADNESS

The experience of self-compassion is one in which I allow. I actually let in and become vulnerable to what previously was intolerable. I let in the information from life without judging it, without interpreting it. In the quotation at the beginning of this chapter, Steven Harrison asks, "Can we see directly into what our experience is without trying to modify it, improve it, change it, or condition it?" I want to be able to see and face what's going on in life and in the world. I want to be able to let it in. When I am able to let in all of life, it touches my heart and breaks my heart open.

Living with a broken-open heart is allowing myself to feel the natural grief or pain that can result from feeling something that was previously intolerable. Opening myself to feel this grief vulnerably is to face it with my heart and with my body. This kind of pain is a natural feeling, a sacred feeling. The practice of grief and mourning is essential to maintaining and dwelling in the flow of my life.

Mourning is a celebration of the aliveness within my sadness. It is a practice that moves me toward equanimity, a consciousness without preference for one feeling experience over another. When I am in this state of equanimity, I am connected to the aliveness at the heart of both happiness and sadness.

Moving toward pain and feeling grief is not an easy practice for most of us, and sometimes it gets very difficult for me, too. When this happens, I make a deliberate effort to spend time with myself or to receive support in the loving presence of another person. The more I allow myself to feel intensity, the more I am able to be with the fullness of the energy within any situation in life. When I can be with the fullness, I am brought in touch with the beauty of life in the pain. In touch with this beauty, I become a vehicle for spirit and life rather than an obstruction to it.

## MEDITATION

### *Opening to Uncertainty*

**This meditation and the journaling practice that follows offer statements and questions as inquiries for inner exploration. Each of these is an invitation to connect to what arises in you as you receive it. Allow yourself to explore your inner experiencing in response to the question rather than trying to answer the question definitively. If something arises and you can't connect to it, that's okay. Just allow it.**

**You might want to record the following meditation first and then play it to guide you. Invite yourself to spend time with and notice whatever is present after each question or reflection.**

---

Let's begin.

I invite you to bring your attention to your body and to your breath. Relax and breathe.

Notice any feelings or sensations that you're experiencing.

Just allow the attention to simply and gently rest on your inner experience, your breathing, your feelings, and your sensations. Just be with them.

I invite you to notice within yourself the nature of change and how you meet it.

Notice if there is resistance to change, if there is part of you that wants to control life, that calls for certainty. When we hear that voice, we want to listen deeply to it—not to believe it but to listen for the precious life that is longed for. As you bring compassion to this part, can you become curious about it?

Stay with your experience and allow the possibility of welcoming discomfort.

Can you let go of your need for safety and security?

Can you welcome the uncertainty of what is to come?

You can use the compassion practices of "I can be patient," "I don't need to push myself," and "I can breathe."

From this place of compassion, can you imagine embracing the unknown and being at peace with insecurity?

Take time to breathe.

Be with the life that is flowing within you in this moment.

Can you open yourself to embracing the next moment?

Can you rest into trust in yourself?

Can you rest into trusting life?

Relaxing into the center of your Being, breathe and feel.

## JOURNAL

## *Embracing All of Life*

**These questions are offered as further inquiries for inner exploration. They are within the realm of our relationship to experience. Some of these questions are very general, so if something specific comes up, allow it to come up.**

**If you are practicing with another person, your partner can ask the questions and then wait as a silent witness while you share your responses aloud to each question.**

---

Let's begin.

I invite you to bring your attention to your body and to your breath. Relax and breathe.

Now, regarding your whole life, how do you resist your experience of life? Notice one way you resist your experience of life.

In your relationships, what kind of expectations do you have of others and of life?

How are you attached to outcome? You can think of one or several examples.

How do you hold on to pleasure and avoid painful experiences?

Can you imagine embracing and feeling okay with the unexpected?

Can you imagine growing in your capacity to embrace unmet needs and to relax your avoidance of pain?

Can you rest into trust in yourself and in life?

Though the questions in this meditation and journaling practice are unique, they are related to each other in a theme of allowing, focusing on the different nuances or aspects of allowing and not resisting. Each question is new and fresh, but if some similarity between them arises, allow it to arise.

---

There is a simplicity in mystery that simply says, "I don't know." And when I say, "I don't know," a spaciousness arises within me and in the relational field between me and another.

CHAPTER SIX

# Mourning and Celebration

> It is only through letting our heart break that we discover something unexpected: The heart cannot actually break, it can only break open. . . . To live with a broken-open heart is to experience life full-strength. . . . When the heart breaks open, it marks the beginning of a real love affair with this world. It is a broken-hearted love affair, rather than the conventional kind based on hope and expectation. Only in this fearless love that can respond to life's pain as well as its beauty can we be of real help to ourselves or anyone else in this difficult age.
>
> —JOHN WELWOOD[13]

FOR ME, living with my heart open means living from my vulnerability and a willingness to engage all the experiences of life as fully as I can. To the extent I can live in this openhearted way, I am living in a flow of energetic movement, of coming and going.

The psychologist and teacher John Welwood's words point to what I call "living in the heart of gratitude and grief." Gratitude and grief are not opposites; they are a spectrum. (Note that I'm using the term *grief* synonymously with *mourning*.) As I receive life in any moment, it can bring me the fullness of something I am grateful for, something that nurtures my heart, something wonderful or beautiful that I can take in and that links me to my heart. At the very next moment, I can experience something I do not enjoy, something that stimulates pain or difficulty or grief in me. If I want to remain with my heart open, I must be able to receive whatever is difficult for me to experience with a *broken-open* heart.

Living with an open heart brings a particular challenge. So much of our culture and social conditioning have taught us to protect ourselves from emotional pain, to keep our hearts from breaking open. However, to receive an experience in an undefended, open way, I must be vulnerable to it. When I am vulnerable to the pain of an unmet need, what arises in me is natural pain, which is often natural grief or mourning. When I experience natural pain, it is not a contracted experience or one in which I am in a suffering state.

Natural pain links me to my heart. The pain itself reminds me that something matters to me, something is dear to me, something is precious to me. It invites me—even if I can't do it immediately—to be vulnerable and open myself to this natural ache I feel when I experience a dissonance with something I deeply value. I believe that opening to mourning is an essential part of a spiritual practice. This is living with a *broken-open* heart.

## LIVING WITH AN OPEN HEART

Mourning is a celebration of the aliveness within my sadness and my happiness. It's a practice that moves me toward equanimity, a consciousness without preference for one state over another. This principle is essentially very simple but profound, as it calls us into an ongoing practice of living with an open heart: *I want to meet life equally, no matter what it is.* I always aspire to practice this principle, even if I can't do it at every moment.

I want to remain awake, because otherwise I fall into a kind of unconscious, automatic trance of not being as present as I enjoy being. In the midst of the ever-moving, ever-changing flow of life, I want to stop and savor a moment, whether I am experiencing enjoyment, gratitude, or an energy of pain. When what I am experiencing is discomfort, the principle I want to remember over and over again is that pain is an energy that links me to something that matters to me. I don't feel emotional or psychological pain about something that doesn't matter to me, that I don't value.

The nature of this work of Living Compassion is to celebrate through gratitude when something in life nurtures me and opens my heart in joy, peace, fun, love, or whatever the quality is—that first stream. I also want to invite my heart into the second stream of Living Compassion and to be open with challenging experiences. When I am able to do this, I can celebrate the life within the mourning, and I can stay in a flow so that even when I feel grief, I feel aliveness.

## RECOGNIZING WHAT IS PRECIOUS

I use the term *precious* to describe something that is dear to me, something I deeply value. It is a word I often use in my gratitude and mourning practices. Stating what is precious to me in any moment helps me to move intentionally into an openhearted relationship with life. If there is something I value in the exterior world, I want to name it with inspired thought, consciously. If I feel gratitude, I want to go deeper, to take my time to explore my experience of it and to identify what is precious to me.

A gratitude practice can be a mindful, moment-by-moment exploration. I can deliberately choose one moment and identify what I enjoy in my exterior life. For example, I pause and notice something in the natural world, perhaps the quiet breeze, the sun shining, a beautiful environment. Or maybe I notice some animal I enjoy or a person who has said or done something that touched me. Whatever it is, I slow down and say to myself, "This is precious to me," as I receive it inwardly in my body.

When I experience interiorly what is exteriorly precious *to* me, what is awakened is something precious *in* me. This is experienced as a feeling, an energy, a quality that is felt in my body, in my heart. I feel the physical sensation of it, and it has a beauty and a radiance. When I feel the external beauty as it resides in the internal beauty, it occurs to me that it is the beauty of my heart that can recognize the beauty that's in the world. I want to remember these two different elements of life experience: the exterior *to* me and the interior *in* me. These are the two parts of my approach to gratitude and mourning.

Saying "This is precious *in* me" connects me with the quality of a need or value that I sense as an energy. For example, if the need is enjoyment, I may experience a quality of warmth, or a quality of peaceful, quiet, joy, or even a sense of exhilaration that comes from humor mixed with enjoyment. Whatever the energy is, I take it in. I feel the physical sensations in my body.

When I examine my interior experience of "preciousness"—and this is likely to be a different bodily experience each time—several aspects become clear. There is an emotional quality I feel, a resonance. There is an interbeing that happens in my relationship to all of life. As I recognize and let in what is precious *to* me, what is precious *in* me awakens the beauty and radiance I feel in my body. I experience this as being fed by life. It is a nurturing that feeds my soul.

## LIBERATING THE ENERGY CAUGHT IN SUFFERING

There are many obstacles to experiencing grief and also to experiencing gratitude. If I close myself off from feeling pain, I also close myself off from feeling joy. Both pain and joy require openheartedness and vulnerability.

One of the things that makes it difficult to experience pain is that most of us have an orientation toward it as something negative. Of course, this attitude is learned. It comes from what we've established through our own life experiences and from the cultural messages that reinforce the orientation that "pain is bad, and pleasure is good." So we gravitate toward pleasure, hang on to it, grasp it, and have a hard time letting it go when there is a natural change. We experience some pain and want to avoid it, push it away, and try to manage and control it.

Our suffering is a function of the stories we tell ourselves, whether we consciously recognize them or not. Our narratives are the source of our suffering, and they are created by thoughts that are usually unconscious and automatic, such as "It shouldn't be this way!" or "Why can't it be easy?" or other variations of these. When we are identified and fused with this kind of thinking, it becomes beliefs through which we filter life. When we are fused with this kind of thinking, one way to look at it is that we're not fully in life. We're separated, as though we're floating above life in this mental sphere that is only allowing us a limited range of experience.

When I experience the pain and suffering of contraction and reactive thinking, I want to remember that this is an opportunity, that there is an opening, and that this is actually the way to beauty. However, it may not necessarily be easy to remember this, because it's easy to get lost and collapse into what the mind calls horrible, horrific, terrible, or unacceptable. The second stream practice of Living Compassion draws us to always remember that there is another possibility: that compassion liberates the energy caught in suffering.

## APPROACHING PAIN WITH AWARENESS AND COMPASSION

When there is something that stimulates pain in me, I want to recognize what happens automatically within my consciousness. Can I notice that I'm shying away from my discomfort? Do I notice if I am projecting my pain onto the environment or the other person? Am I judging them with my expectations or my disappointments?

Being with grief is a practice of self-compassion or inner compassion. It is oriented toward a particular way of being with life when it takes the form of grief. So, as in all of my self-compassion practices, the first thing I want to do is to pause and then bring my consciousness to the pain I am experiencing. I want to have an intention to approach the pain with awareness rather than to move away from it.

The practice of inner compassion is one of noticing and allowing whatever pain or grief arises to be there. I give that contracted experience space, and this begins the process. The pain or grief starts unfolding, so what is underneath it eventually reveals itself. Maybe more pain or grief is revealed. Perhaps reactive feelings surface or the protective, defensive part of the mind is triggered, and there is reactive thinking. As the process unfolds, I name and acknowledge whatever I notice. It may take time to stay with my experience and process this.

Besides pausing, breathing, and creating a spacious presence within myself, what this grief practice requires is connecting with a caring attention. This tender attention will help me notice if I am moving away from this experience. Everything in my history has taught me that I should do anything other than stay with grief or any other form of pain. However, the more I practice turning toward the pain with tenderness, curiosity, and awareness, the more I can become familiar with the patterned tendencies of how I experience life, how I avoid it, and how I attempt to grasp it.

When I can touch the preciousness of what I am grieving, there is a healing that takes place within me. I may still feel the tenderness of the pain, but it is an openhearted grief that touches the beauty within the unfulfilled need. If I'm not touching the beauty in my experience, I'm not fully grieving. I'm not in my experience in the fullness of the grief. That doesn't mean I have to feel the beauty, but it's an indication for me to acknowledge the beauty.

## AN UNENDING GRATITUDE PRACTICE

The simple acknowledgment that something is precious to me has been very important in helping me to engage in living with gratitude. When I don't acknowledge what is valuable to me, I recognize that perhaps I am taking for granted the fact that I live in a home, I have shelter, I have food, I live with quiet, I live with a partner who is supportive of me, and we have a quality of relationship that is nurturing. I have these animal friends of mine, furry creatures that walk around the house and sometimes do things that are annoying and sometimes do things that are delightful. I can enjoy going outside even if it's raining and gray. There is this existence that I move through in awareness; I breathe and feel my aliveness.

When I engage in this practice of gratitude, I notice it is unending. There is a never-ending recognition and appreciation for so much of life. I get to the place where it is all precious to me. This may be difficult to understand, but even the pain is precious, even the difficulty is precious. When I am awake and I emerge into this space of gratitude, suddenly everything is vibrant; everything is alive. Everything, even pain, is alive. I've touched these moments, and they are exhilarating because they take me beyond my conditioned mind, which is constantly evaluating what is good and what is bad, what is right and what is wrong. The practice of living with an open heart invites gratitude; it even welcomes the experience we call pain.

So as I take in all of life, moment by moment, what awakens in me? What arises in me? This inquiry practice draws my attention to feel fully what is stirring in me. It draws me to look at and notice the thoughts and stories that are going through my mind. Can I acknowledge them and see that they are products of my mind in reaction rather than inspired thoughts that reflect some projected reality that is true?

My heart is my guide in life. What I value and what I care about are the guidelines that help me to connect to those qualities that are inherent in my life. I am responsible for staying in tune with what I am needing and what I am valuing. I want to speak and act from that place of awareness rather than from a place in which I am not connected to my heart or in harmony with what I care about and value.

## MEDITATION

# *Gratitude*

**When we experience gratitude, we feel thankful for something. When we celebrate life (whether in gratitude or mourning), there is an inner resonance we feel with our needs or values. Connecting with the qualities of our needs, we can dwell in their beauty and fullness.**

---

Let's begin.

Bring your attention to your body and to your breath. Relax and breathe.

Now name something in the outer world that you are grateful for (an event, something someone did, or something you observed).

Name what you are feeling emotionally as you consider this experience you are grateful for. Notice how you are experiencing your body energy, and the value or need that was fulfilled—what is precious *to* you.

Feel and experience the precious longing or qualities of the need that is awakened in you. Feel it, dwell in it. Name what is precious *in* you.

Encompass and hold both the outer stimulus and inner experience together. Sit with this as long as you have time to.

Wherever you finish this practice, end by relaxing into the center of your Being, breathing, and feeling.

You may want to journal your gratitude experience or share it with your partner, if you are doing this meditation with someone else.

## JOURNAL

### *The Beauty and Energy Within Mourning*

**In an undefended experience of grief or mourning, there is a loss, an unfulfilled need or value, and the inner experience linked to that longing. What accompanies grief and mourning are deep feelings of sadness, disheartenment, or similar vulnerable feelings that are felt as a sweet pain.**

**The invitation in this practice is to take time to notice and allow to unfold what is underneath or inside the pain. When we touch into the energy of the unfulfilled need, there's a preciousness to it. There's a beauty in this energy. We want to take our time to stay with the beauty of our need and to feel it fully.**

**If you are doing this practice alone, you might want to record the questions first and then play your recording, pausing to receive and then respond to each one. You may want to note your responses to the questions in your journal.**

**If you are processing with another person, your partner can ask the questions and then wait as a silent witness while you share your responses to each question out loud.**

---

Let's begin.

I invite you to bring your attention to your body and to your breath. Relax and breathe.

Now name something in the outer world—an event or something that someone did or said—that was not in harmony with what you value or need.

Name what you are feeling emotionally, your body energy, and the value or need that was not fulfilled. Name what is precious to you.

What are the thoughts you have about this experience? What is the story?

Feel whatever pain, disheartenment, or sadness resonates in this experience.

Feel and sense inside of this feeling of pain. What are you longing for? Allow any sadness or mourning that arises. Invite it. Listen to it.

What is precious in you?

Enter into the full embodiment of the beauty of your need and dwell in the fullness of what is precious in you and absent in your experience.

Take time to bring your awareness back and, when you are ready, write about your experience in your journal or share your experience with your partner.

---

There is a difference between experiencing the deficiency of needs and mourning the beauty of an unmet need. When I experience deficiency, there is always thinking involved. When mourning the beauty of an unmet need, my awareness is on my heart, and I feel the natural pain that always touches something held with beauty and honored. Mourning always includes a celebration, which is a form of gratitude. Celebration and mourning are both ways of acknowledging our aliveness and our relationship to the life flow.

CHAPTER SEVEN

# Living the Divine

Think about the difference this makes in a relationship: "I don't want your love. I want the same love you want. I don't want your love. I want what you want, and we can find It together and share our deepening experience of It. I thought it was your love I wanted, and it hurt so much when you couldn't give it. I even made a bargain that if I gave it to you, I could expect it back. I thought you agreed to this bargain. I thought you were part of the deal.

I lived in fear that your love would disappear. I moved so deeply into the veil. Now I hear within me the whispering of something else. I feel the possibility of a Love that has nothing to do with you—an infinite resource that is always there. This Love is not affected by any condition, nor does it change in the stream of time. It is the same Love whether my body is strong or weak, whether I am rich and bountiful in material things or whether I am poor. It is not affected by things of this world. This is the Love that brings release. This is the Love that dissolves chains. This is the Love that brings peace. This is the only Love I want. It releases you, my friend, from all our contracts.

—STEPHEN SCHWARTZ[14]

Our work of Living Compassion emanates from the vision of infinite, mysterious, total, absolute love coming through the human heart. It is the work of how we, with the mystery of our individuality, can be with ourselves and with each other. It is the holy, sacred, beautiful life work of approaching the knot of fear within us and with each other compassionately, and it requires a tremendous amount of courage.

When I experience a certain quality of connection with someone and there is a sense of deep love alive in me and in the other person, the words "You met my need for love" no longer express my experience. It is more that through our connection, our relationship has become a conduit for divine energy. In full compassionate mutuality, we activate the potential for divine energy, which we both experience as this warmth of love. We invoke the divine energy to come and be present in our relationship. What was transcendent we have made immanent. The light in me and the light in you touches and creates another light, even if it is momentary.

Many words are used to express the Divine: *God* and *Spirit* are among them. We can experience the reality of the Divine in many ways. When I bring a loving attention to life (to my inner life or to you), that is the Divine manifesting. When there is kindness, that is the Divine. When there are acceptance and love, the Divine is manifesting. In my experience, the Divine goes beyond religion. Although we can use religious approaches to help us connect to the Divine, I don't think the Divine has any kind of religious affiliation.

## CHOOSING LIFE

One of the ways that this mysterious life force that we call the Divine expresses through us is in our authentic choices. It is as if God is speaking to us continually in the background, saying "Remember me . . . you can remember me through your choices and by always being true to yourself." Remembering this has been the highest priority in my life.

I always want to choose what might serve everyone best, but I never know—I make mistakes. However, I don't want to make the mistake of not taking action.

Life moves forward; it expresses. It is a radiant phenomenon; it shines. Each human being also shines. I shine. You shine. We shine as a state of our essential Being. But there's something about this shining that is enhanced by stepping forward and taking action. How we step forward is important. We are conditioned to want to know, analyze, plan, and strategize. Our brain tries to dominate, and we feel compelled to understand or predict the outcome of our actions before we take them. This conditioning is something we will need to relinquish. In contrast, we want to step forward from the place of receptivity, inclusiveness, and compassion. Action that manifests the Divine comes from a deep force within us, and we are drawn forward to act, to meet and engage with life. Although our dreams, visions, and intentions may be shaped by our lives, they are sourced by the unnamable life force, by that which is radiant in life and radiates life itself.

What's always present is our ability to choose our actions while remembering to be true to ourselves, to be authentic and real. I want to remember that the one who chooses is not the *I* who is a person and a personality but the deeper *I* who senses the life force. When we are in contact with the life force, our life and relationships become a creation, not in isolation but as cocreators with the other people and groups in our life.

## IN RELATIONSHIP WITH EACH OTHER AND ALL OF LIFE

To be in life fully requires both the fullness of freedom and the fullness of love. What do I mean by freedom? For me, freedom isn't "from" or "to" anything or anyone. It is the very nature of essential Being that we are. We cannot achieve freedom because it is already the given condition of our Being. When I am aware that I am free, I can see others and recognize others in their true state of freedom. Then and only then can I say "I see you" in the deepest way. This is where divine presence comes alive in relationship.

I am not able to be in a loving relationship unless both of us are absolutely free. Without freedom, we are acting out of the sense of obligation, acting on some contractual basis like that described by Stephen at the beginning of this chapter: "If you do this for me, then I will love you" and "If you don't do this for me, then you do not love me." This kind of contract—I will feel loved only if you act a certain way—is not free. When we choose to act and speak in harmony with what we truly value, what truly matters to us, then we are living in the energy of freedom.

Whatever we experience within is always a response to how we are in relationship to all of life. Probably the simplest way to regard this is that as human beings, we receive life input in terms of relationship. We metabolize life information, experience it, and digest it. If we receive information from another human being that is difficult or painful for us, then we can transform it within ourselves so that what we give back isn't more of the same, more reactivity. When we distill the experience of needs being fulfilled, we are taken to the essence of the self—the essential Being that is always here in what we live and feel—and there's a sense of coming home to who we really are.

Nonviolent Communication is the best approximation I know of right now that attempts to actualize the Divine, together, in relationship. We all have a deep yearning that goes beyond words, not for something outside of us but for a resonance of something deep that's alive in all of us and that we yearn to activate and enjoy with one another.

Why does it feel so good to have our needs met and fulfilled? Why does it feel so good to have a quality of connection in which my defenses and your defenses fall away, and we simply meet in the undefended warmth and joy and radiance of love and cocreativity? The basic divine impulse in life is to actualize, to be born. So, for me, the reason it feels so good when my needs are fulfilled is because I am reconnected to the basic impulse of life. The construct of human needs is a vehicle that supports me in seeing you through the deepest values of the qualities that you express and in expressing mine. When your need is met in relation to me, I am meeting not just your need; I am meeting your essential Being,

It isn't always experienced that way. This conscious, full, clear recognition of the essence of me and you is fairly rare. What is important is to see that there is a pathway to experiencing the nature of what life actually is. We are living and practicing this pathway when I see you in your need and you see me in my need. Love is the actualization and lived energy of the comingling of each of our separate selves.

The reason Nonviolent Communication is ultimately and only a spiritual process is that it is a way in which you and I, individually and collectively, can come to behold each other as who and what we really are. The process, premises, and principles of Nonviolent Communication and of Living Compassion provide a means for moving through apparent disconnection and conflict and paving the way to eventually experiencing the reality of communion.

## INSTRUMENTS OF THE DIVINE

A lot of the spiritual, esoteric traditions offer some version of self-realization, self-transcendence, or enlightenment. For me, that is only part of the picture, and what completes it is not self-realization but coming to communion. A metaphor I like to use is that a human being is an instrument or a vehicle for living and expressing the Divine, the life force. Our work of Living Compassion can be said to be like cultivating, developing, and honing our instrument.

If an instrument is out of tune, it doesn't play to its highest potential; it plays a distortion. Using this metaphor, if we are playing a note and it is distorted through the mind, this happens because our instrument hasn't been fine-tuned enough. When we differentiate what is going on in our thinking, we create an open space that fine-tunes our instrument so that it can receive and express the actual energies we transmit to and from one another.

The twofold spiritual practice of Living Compassion I've shared throughout this book supports us in cultivating, growing, dwelling in, and becoming more capable of embodying the passion of these energies: the actualization of how love and trust live in us, how the experience of belonging in relationship and in community lives in us. The more we live the radiance, peace, and creativity that are the very qualities of the self, the stronger our instrument becomes, and we can play the song of our being more clearly to each other. Through hearing each other with compassion, we support each other in fine-tuning our instrument so that it plays the music of our Being in a beautiful way. We begin to embody the energies of the life force together.

## COMMUNION

The central part of this work of Living Compassion can be seen as entering more fully in life itself. When I am attuned to life and there is another person present with me and for me, this magical, sacred space is created. One human being and another human being are holding each other in a shared space where we can welcome our own and each other's experience without judgment, without reservation. The specificity of language that the Nonviolent Communication process teaches can be a conduit for the full flowing of life energy and the transformation of whatever obstructs it. For me, the most important aspect of NVC is the concept of universal human needs. They are what links us to our essence. Approaching our authenticity through our needs can support us in giving meaning to the way we are with ourselves and the intentionality with which we approach our relationships.

When we get to the heart of who we are as human beings, we all yearn for a simple, tender way of being with one another. The beauty of this work of Living Compassion is that it brings me to this place where I experience a profound recognition that we are all the same at the deepest human level. There is a universality of the flow of life within, how we connect with the world, and how we encounter the obstacles to the life force. I want to connect to life as it flows through me so that

I can connect to life as it flows through you. It is the same life that is flowing through both of us.

When we are communicating with each other, what we communicate is our internal reality. When someone is speaking, they are speaking their heart: the qualities, the care, and the pain of whatever is in their heart. It's not that the content and form of what we say don't matter, only that they are indicators of these realities. There is fullness and a beauty in this reality. We can ask ourselves, "Are we listening to this person share what's truly in them? What is their heart really communicating?" This is like a meditation practice where we focus our attention on the essential living energy in ourselves and in the other person.

*Communion* is another word for the intimate connection we can experience together as a practice and as a way of living. For communion to occur, it is necessary to create an open space within myself in relation to the other person. The fullness of this communion or full mutuality is that we are no longer identified with the sense of our separation because we are meeting in this place where the life in you and the life in me equally matter to each other. It's almost as if it's not *my needs* and *your needs* as a separate, personal reality but that we are connected in a field where it's just *the need*; the life energy is here manifesting in this phenomenon that appears to be you and me. On one level, there is a *you* and a *me*—we don't lose the sense of our personal identity. But something is unified when we have this special, wonderful kind of meeting with someone in which our personal identity softens or loosens, and there's just a field of energy that we share.

The life in me and the life in you come from the same source, which is divine life energy. We are in relationship all the time, whether we are in direct relationship with another person or not. We exist as "unity in relationship" with everything. With awareness of the wholeness of the world comes the awareness that my needs and your needs matter. Mutuality flowers from this awareness.

The quality, nature, and shape of our lives is entirely dependent on how we meet the life force within and between us. How we choose to meet the life force can open us to the mystery within it. I always want to remember that the essence of any expression—no matter how hard it is to hear—is actually life itself. I want to remember that every expression is life calling for life. When I can experience this not as a mental concept but in a fully felt, bodily-relaxed stance, this is the living essence of nonviolence, of real compassion.

One way to describe this experience is that we are transforming an "I-it" to an "I-thou" relationship in which we have an unmediated, direct experience of the other rather than through our judgments and projections. In the I-thou relationship, a concept developed by the philosopher Martin Buber,[15] we discover that we have the same basic life energy flowing through us, the same qualities that give us meaning. We all want to be seen, we all value support, and we all thrive when there is honesty and authenticity. Something happens to us as human beings; something comes alive when these qualities are active in our relationships. We enter into the energy of love. When we align ourselves with the consciousness and language that supports the energy of love, we move from awareness of separation to awareness of connection.

Although our communication exchange doesn't connect us per se, language inspired by presence helps us remove the obstacles of separation so we can experience the already existing unity. We call this "connection" in NVC. Living this integration and embodiment of the "I" and "we," there's a longing and a way of tapping into and communicating our wholeness so that we can meet another human being in the relational space in our wholeness. This is embodying the qualities of our Being in relationship. We experience an I-thou relationship. It is the communion of differentiated unity in the "you" and the "me."

We are growing the qualities that make it possible for us to live into those energies that manifest when we are in communion. One moment of authenticity, one moment of love, one moment of seeing the shining in someone's eyes and feeling the radiance and warmth in my heart is a moment in which the Divine is manifested . . . in just that one moment.

## AN EARLY AWAKENING

I want to share an experience I had as a boy that opened my awareness to the vastness and beauty of the Divine.

One fairly ordinary summer evening when I was about eleven, being bored with television, I walked aimlessly out into the front yard. The night sky seemed exceptionally clear and filled with stars. I spontaneously opened my mind and began to wonder, "Where does it end?" My consciousness started to go out into the stars. "Where does it end?" I don't think I'd ever thought about it before. My mind went up into the night sky and my awareness seemed to get carried by my wondering. It was more than an intellectual wondering: The very essence of my Being was in a state of deep wonder. It seemed as though my consciousness kept going and going, far out into the night sky and into the depths of space. At some point, I could not envision an end, and I was overcome with a distinct clarity that there was no end.

Abruptly, something happened: It was as though something deep inside snapped or shifted and I was transported to a place of sudden realization. A recognition came to me that was absolutely and utterly surprising, powerful, and clear. What struck me had to do with who I was and the word *always* came to me. It became utterly clear, utterly self-evident that who I was in my very essence and at the core of my Being always was and always would be. I suddenly knew without a doubt that "I always was, and I always will be." It was absolutely clear and absolutely self-evident. It was the most profound truth that I have ever experienced.

That evening I stayed in a magical state of awe for several hours. Given my eleven-year-old mind, I was dumbstruck. I was in a world I could never have previously imagined. I had no words at the time to help make sense of the experience. I could only rest in the awakening itself, wondering about and questioning all of life. It was so clear and obvious that the sense of who I am always existed and always will exist, that I began to wonder why everyone else wasn't acting from this truth or even talking about it. Observing that no one ever talked about this—this sense of absolute truth—I intuited that no one would believe me nor be interested if I spoke about it. Strangely, I never talked about it. I did not have the intellectual capacity then to understand that my realization about my essence was something that existed beyond time and space.

Something shifted in me forever that night. The indelible truth I opened to has stayed, residing in me as a profound knowing: a powerfully comforting, deeply peaceful knowing. And yet this glimpse into such ultimate truth also brought with it a fundamental yearning and longing to understand how to fit something so expansive meaningfully into daily life. What came to me from the earliest of my spiritual practices and based on that early awakening was not that I want realization or liberation; rather, I want to live the truth. I want to fully embody and live this magnificence in life.

## OPENING THE CHANNEL TO EACH OTHER

One of the beauties of Nonviolent Communication is that it integrates the Eastern mystical tradition and Western psychological, interpersonal communication. This integration allows us this spiritual orientation for approaching human needs. NVC and Living Compassion practices cultivate an awareness of needs and open the channels between us so we can release any obstacles to enjoying the energy of the Divine. This integration helps us to find and live our already existing unity.

Many years ago, when I entered my adult life, I immediately began a spiritual and life quest that took the forms of spiritual practice and the study of psychology and communication. My quest ever since has been the integration of these two. Each of these approaches has its richness, but they are incomplete unless I'm integrating them. I've found a necessary consciousness available in the spiritual and mystical traditions. And yet unless I can live this consciousness in my relationships using language in the space of mutuality, then unity consciousness isn't necessarily helpful to me, particularly when there's disconnection.

Connected with the divine energy within, I want to bring this energy to my relationships. I'm conscious that other people have their own agency. I don't have choice over what they experience, but I can influence them. I can bring an energy, a presence, and an understanding to our relationship. To the degree that I do this, I am living the Divine. It is not an abstraction that is only available to me in special cases. I can bring it into all my relationships. This, for me, is the essence of life. It is the beauty of one human being with another human being creating the space between us. This is where all the magic happens. This is where the sacred resides.

What has become increasingly important to me is to explore more deeply and to share with others this space where we meet in authenticity and mutuality. This space can be a profoundly healing one. There can be something deeply sacred in witnessing and being witnessed. In this relational space, I reach outside of myself and both vulnerably share and vulnerably receive. As I receive the other, I suspend my reality for a moment and take in their reality. I take in the world as if I am receiving them the way that they experience themselves.

One of the most powerful tools for spiritual growth and healing in relationship I've experienced in my life has been the Dyad Meditation Process.[16] The Enlightenment Intensive[17] on which it is based was the very first practice I learned when I was nineteen or twenty years old. This process creates an unconventional intimacy in which two human beings can meet in vulnerability and with open hearts. A dyad is a pair—two people who are sitting and facing each other, attending to each other, taking turns every five minutes either to share or witness. Through the forty-minute practice, a quality of depth develops in connection, presence, and awareness.

There are two roles in the Dyad Meditation Process. The first role is the witness. The witness asks a question and then stays completely silent for the entire practice, offering soft but constantly available eye contact, if possible. At the end of each five minutes, the witness says, "Thank you."

The second role is the sharing person. This person brings their awareness to their inner life and then shares what arises in their experience as they receive each question from the witness.

This practice is an invitation to show up just as we are with one another as openhearted human beings in an undefended intimacy. This is a spiritual practice without dogma; it is a practice of simple presence with the beauty of the human heart. It creates a place where we meet each other in spiritual companionship.

The Dyad Meditation Process is a simple way to help remove the veil that obscures the consciousness of the heart. In this process, we are reminded of this sacred space where two hearts meet and the Divine emerges. Life is waiting for us to come together and meet in this space of presence where we are already undivided.

If, while connecting with another person, such as during the Dyad Meditation Process, a longing arises that is related to some deep relational wounding—for example, if that wounding is around trust—it can be challenging to connect with the longing for trust because the trauma carries so much pain of trust not being fulfilled. If you are not able to access the fullness of trust, then this is an indication that whatever arises is there to be embraced with acceptance and compassion. I have found that the sacred process of witnessing in mutuality is an important part of a spiritual practice, and it is important for healing. Something that became evident to me a long time ago is that relational wounds can only be healed in relationship.

I think it's an incredibly important aspect of this work to acknowledge that what we are doing is not an easy practice for most of us. This work needs support. It can be either inner support or external support. If I don't have the capacity to offer myself internal support, then I want to remember the possibility of receiving external support in the form of a loving presence—someone willing to accompany me without judging me, who can create a space of kindness and welcome into it whatever I am experiencing. The pain I am holding within myself only yields into a space of kindness. That space of kindness is essential for development and healing.

## MEDITATION

### *Connecting to the Collective Human Heart*

**You might want to record this meditation first and then play your recording. Remember to move slowly through the meditation. If you are doing this with a partner, that person can read the meditation to you, pausing for you to be with each invitation, and then exchanging roles when you are complete.**

**If you are doing the meditation alone, you may want to journal your experience when you have finished.**

---

Let's begin.

So much of meditation and life is about attention, the quality of directed awareness. Bring your attention to your awareness, your experiencing, both inner and outer. Bring your attention to your breathing and be with it with simple awareness.

Relax and breathe.

I invite you to tune in to the collective field of humanity, the collective human heart.

Bring your attention to just breathing and sense bringing all of us together, all on this planet.

By attending to the quality of your attention, it can grow.

Breathe in and receive this field of collective humanity. Bring all the experiences, the suffering, the limitation, the newfound joys . . . bring it all into your heart.

Take it in with love and compassion, with an open heart . . . and breathe out more love and compassion.

Breathing in the experience of all humanity, breathing out strength, love, and presence, offering this love and presence from your heart to all of life.

Breathing in, allowing your heart to be open, tender, and vulnerable . . . and breathing out, feeling openness, warmth, joy, and belonging on this earth.

Feel the presence, the subtlety of life all around and in you. It is always here.

As you open your eyes, enter life in a different way.

## JOURNAL

## *Living in the Energy of Compassion*

**This practice has more value than just as an exercise; it is an invitation to dwell in the energies of compassion and authenticity (or whatever needs you choose). This practice cultivates the embodiment of these energies of your aliveness and keeps you centered on what really matters to you.**

**You might want to record the steps to this practice first and then play your recording. Remember to move slowly through the suggestions. If you cannot connect with the fullness of the need, then the invitation is to bring compassion to those parts of you that are in resistance. If you are practicing with a partner, that person can read the questions to you, pausing for you to explore each step, and then exchanging roles when you are complete.**

**If you are practicing alone, you may want to journal your experience with each of the steps, or you can make notes in your journal at the end of this practice.**

---

Let's begin.

Bring your attention to your body and to your breath. Relax and breathe.

I invite you to explore how the quality of compassion lives in you. Begin by accessing a memory, remembering as vividly as you can a time when you experienced compassion . . . when you were feeling this energy of compassion.

Connect to what compassion feels like, how it feels to live in the energy of compassion. Notice its felt qualities . . . let yourself embody compassion or, if there is any resistance, bring compassion to that.

Sense how living in the energy of compassion feels in your body.

Allow yourself to sink into this feeling, into its energy. Allow whatever arises to be there.

Is there a moving forward in your inner experiencing?

Is there any sense of an expanded self, an encompassing presence, in which the different parts of you belong and feel more whole in this moment?

Dwell in the experience as long as you have time. When you are ready, you can complete this practice by journaling about your exploration.

---

Spirituality, as I see it, integrates the two streams of Living Compassion: one that flows inward, nurturing our self-compassion and awareness; and the other that flows outward, allowing us to embody compassion in our relationships and communities. The personal, inward-facing stream touches on self-realization, and the outward-facing relational stream is about compassionate presence with others. Together these form a complete spiritual life practice.

When I am fully living in the quality of compassion, I become compassion. My identity is no longer living in those identifications of life experiences in which I am experiencing fear, tension, anger, and separation. This is what I see as all of the work of Living Compassion.

A spiritual life practice can be seen as addressing our relationship with the life force that exists within and outside of us and sweeps us into living experiences. Spirituality is the life in me and the life in you. The quality, the nature, the shape of our lives is entirely dependent on how we meet the life force. How we choose to meet the life force can open us to the mystery within it. The direction and quality of how we allow the life force to sweep us and to flow through us is dependent upon our awareness and the choices we make.

We are spiritual beings. This spiritual dimension is accessible in everyday life, both internally and in relationship. By bringing this dimension of ourselves into relationship, our Beings and our lives are both enriched.

The relationship space where we invite each other into this mutual experience is one in which I show up and you show up in our vulnerable authenticity. This is the field of Rumi's poem:

Out beyond ideas of wrongdoing and rightdoing,
there is a field. I'll meet you there.
When the soul lies down in that grass,
the world is too full to talk about.
Ideas, language, even the phrase "each other"
doesn't make any sense.[18]

This is an actual space where we live with one another. And for me, it is the heart of the Nonviolent Communication process. This is where spirituality lives.

# Afterword

## *Vision and Dream for Living Compassion*

In the many years that I have shared the work of Living Compassion, I have been blessed and inspired by the love and courage I have experienced and witnessed with thousands of people. In March 2020, I received a message from one of them, my dear friend Andie Nagel (formerly Steidl), in which she described a dream she'd had for Living Compassion.

As I received Andie's message, I was struck by the synchronicity of her dream, as the same dream has lived in me for many years. My strong sense of how dreams radiate from the human heart into life is that they are a creative force that comes from the very essence of Life. As I surrender to the energy of love, there is a living intelligence that flows and guides me. As I surrender to the force of life, it brings me more alive. It is as if the energy is a great attractor.

In my vision, I see people all over the world sharing and living compassion. In this vision, we are living in "islands of aliveness and compassion," responding to the deeper dream that lives in the field of life, from our deepest longings, to embody love and compassion. In my experience, one of the central features of compassion is community. We come together with a shared purpose to create spaces in which all of the parts of us—our pain, trauma, joys, and love—are welcome. In this welcoming space, we invoke the Presence of Life, we surrender our fear, and we allow the love that is at the heart of all human experience to emerge.

With love and community,

—ROBERT

# In Gratitude

We are grateful to our friends and colleagues who contributed to seeing *The Spirituality of Nonviolent Communication* through to its first publication in 2022: Bett Farber, Jeff Brown, Mary Scholl, Andie Nagel, Herman Veluwenkamp, Zandra Hughes, Manfred Friedrich, Richard Broadbent, and many others whose support made the first edition of the book a reality.

Our thanks also go to Elke Dobkowitz and Matthias Heidel, who made this second edition of *The Spiritual Path of Nonviolent Communication* possible. It was edited by Lynd Morris, whose work was guided and enhanced by the encouragement and insight of Shambhala editors Samantha Ripley and Beth Frankl. We are also grateful for the invaluable support generously given by Paul Mahon. Much of the new material in this edition is the result of technical expertise provided by David Steigerwald and Dominic Lucia that enabled access to insights contained in Robert's recordings, hundreds of pages of which were painstakingly transcribed by Bett Farber.

Deep gratitude for the loving support and blessings of Robert's wife, Ruth Joy.

# Notes

1 Stephen R. Schwartz, *I Accept in All Gratitude: Cancer, Crisis, and Compassionate Self-Care* (Riverrun Press, 1992), 65.

2 Stephen R. Schwartz, *The Compassionate Presence: Meeting and Greeting a Love That Will Not End* (Riverrun Press, 1988), 227.

3 Matt Licata, posted on his Facebook page, August 18, 2015.

4 Stephen R. Schwartz, *Angelic Dialogues: The Work of Compassionate Self-Care* (Riverrun Press, 1993), 46.

5 Stephen R. Schwartz, "Everything We Feel Is Holy: An Experience of Compassionate Self-Care," recorded session in Valley Cottage, NY, September 1992.

6 Sarah McLean, *The Power of Attention: Awaken to Love and Its Unlimited Potential with Meditation* (Hay House, 2017).

7 Stephen R. Schwartz, *The Prayer of the Body: Compassionate Self-Care and Reclaiming the Sacred Presence, Selected Excerpts from the Work of Stephen Robbins Schwartz*, compiled by Ray I. Minkler (pub. by compiler, 2009). This PDF was originally published on wordpress.com /compassionate-self-care, which is no longer live.

8 Laurence Heller and Aline LaPierre, *Healing Developmental Trauma: How Early Trauma Affects Self-Regulation, Self-Image, and the Capacity for Relationship* (North Atlantic Books, 2012).

9 Steven Harrison, *What's Next After Now? Post-Spirituality and the Creative Life* (Sentient Publications, 2005).

10 Alan Watts, *The Wisdom of Insecurity* (Vintage Books, 2011).

11 Henry Wadsworth Longfellow, "The Poet's Tale; The Birds of Killingworth," in *Tales of a Wayside Inn* (1863).

12 John Green, *Looking for Alaska* (Penguin, 2006).

13 John Welwood, *Love and Awakening: Discovering the Sacred Path of Intimate Relationship* (Harper Perennial, 1997).

14 Stephen R. Schwartz, *The Compassionate Presence: Meeting and Greeting a Love That Will Not End* (Riverrun Press, 1988), 227.

15 Martin Buber, *I and Thou*, trans. Ronald Gregor Smith (T. & T. Clark, 1937).

16 Global Dyad Meditation, https://www.globaldyadmeditation.org.

17 Yoah Wexler, ed., *Enlightenment and the Enlightenment Intensive: 5 Essays by Charles Berner*, vol. 1 (CreateSpace, 2013).

18 Jalaluddin Rumi, excerpted from "A Great Wagon," *Rumi: Selected Poems*, trans. Coleman Barks (Penguin Classics, 2004).

# About the Author

**ROBERT GONZALES's** work of Living Compassion has emerged from more than thirty years of teaching Nonviolent Communication (NVC) and a lifetime of inquiry into the intersection between spirituality and human communication. His influences included Dr. Marshall Rosenberg (founder of Nonviolent Communication), Stephen Schwartz (creator of Compassionate Self-Care), and other spiritual teachers.

Robert received a PhD in clinical psychology in 1989, and he was a practicing therapist for many years. He met Marshall Rosenberg in 1985 and began teaching NVC in 1986. Robert contributed to the work of the Center for Nonviolent Communication (CNVC) as a Certified Trainer, a certification assessor, and as board president. He also cofounded the NVC Training Institute.

Robert founded the Center for Living Compassion in 2000 as a result of what he referred to as "a calling" to focus on, grow, and share his work of Living Compassion. Robert's first book, *Reflections on Living Compassion: Awakening Our Passion and Living in Compassion*, was published in 2015.

In December 2020, Robert articulated his "Vision and Dream" for expanding Living Compassion, and he invited others to join him in bringing this to life. Robert intended this Vision and Dream to be a guide for bringing the Living Compassion community into a global network of connection and mutual support to live and expand compassion throughout the world. More about Robert's Vision and Dream is in the afterword.

Robert's teachings and practices have supported and continue to help thousands of people worldwide to find healing and freedom from suffering, previously unavailable to them. Robert Gonzales left his body near midnight on November 19, 2021.

# About the Publication Team

**LYND MORRIS** was a member of the first LIFE Program Robert Gonzales offered in 2006, and she continued to participate in annual LIFE reunions for the next eleven years. During this time, Lynd assisted Robert in numerous NVC trainings across the United States, and she was an original member of the team that supported him in developing his work of Living Compassion. Lynd became a CNVC-certified trainer in 2009. In addition to developing her own Welcoming LIFE Program, she co-led Living Compassion retreats with Robert, Simone Anliker, and others in 2013 and 2014. "Robert was a teacher, a colleague, and a friend who immeasurably enriched my life and the lives of thousands of other people," writes Lynd. "The insights he shared and the boundless love and presence he transmitted changed the course of my life. May Robert's light continue to shine through this book and through those who are carrying on his legacy." A professional writer for nearly forty years, Lynd lives outside Washington, DC, in the United States.

**FILIPA HOPE** (www.filipahope.com) is a certified NVC trainer, Living Compassion facilitator, and a student of BioGeometry, the physics of quality. Filipa assisted Robert Gonzales in the program on which this book is based, as well as his other online offerings. In addition to attending Robert's LIFE Program in the United States and New Zealand, she assisted Robert at his last LIFE Program in the United States and at other retreats. Filipa was part of the team that supported the publication of Robert's book *Reflections on Living Compassion: Awakening Our Passion and Living in Compassion* in 2015. According to Filipa, "Robert's work guides me to deeper levels of connection with Life and gives me simple practices to cultivate capacities for this direct experience. His teachings that qualities of longings are the doorways to the extrasensory divine connection through resonance have changed my life and called me ever closer to union, shifting my relationship with obstacles to connection: from rejection and entrenchment to liberation through compassion. Robert's Living Compassion has been a complete package for embodying what is most human about myself and others: our essence as Beings of Love and Freedom." Filipa is now working on content for a Living Compassion app. She lives in Hawke's Bay, New Zealand.

**SIMONE ANLIKER** (www.simoneanliker.com) is a certified NVC trainer, a certified Havening Techniques® practitioner and trainer, and a certified NARM Trauma Master Practitioner. In addition to assisting Robert in his Euro-LIFE Program (2010–2014) and his Australia-New Zealand LIFE Program (2014–2015), Simone co-led several international retreats with Robert. She was part of the team that supported the publication of Robert's book *Reflections on Living Compassion: Awakening Our Passion and Living in Compassion* in 2015, and she is the author of *The Power of Dyad Meditation: A New Way of Meditating in Times of Loneliness and Social Stress*, published in 2020. "I had a deep spiritual experience when I met Robert for the first time in 2006," writes Simone. "We met for a short lunch break during one of his retreats in Austria. As we said goodbye, Robert gave me a heartfelt hug that might have lasted just a few seconds and yet to me it felt like an eternity. It was in that moment that I had an inner vision of the universe opening up and I was falling into its embrace. This marked the beginning of many deeply healing and transforming experiences in Robert's presence. Whenever I returned home from one of his retreats, I was changed. I am forever grateful for fifteen years of healing with my dear friend!" Simone lives in Flüeli-Ranft, Switzerland.

**BETT FARBER** has been an NVC teacher and coach since 2004. They began attending Robert's LIFE Program in 2008 and continued to participate in it for the next eleven years, eventually becoming the transcriber for many of the trainings he offered around the world and online. Bett writes, "The learning I derived from this trove of Robert's sharing, coupled with a desire to better live the principles of Living Compassion, prompted me to offer a Beauty of Needs biweekly empathy group that began in 2012 and continues to this day. Providing resources for *The Spirituality of Nonviolent Communication* and supporting that book's further development in *The Spiritual Path of Nonviolent Communication: Living with Compassion, Connection, and Understanding* has been my anchor and a blessing." Bett lives in Peterborough, New Hampshire.